Poisoned Well
of Tradition

Poisoned Well of Tradition

Baptism and worthless rituals in the church

Isaac Mwangi

MINA CHARIOTS PUBLISHERS
A division of Mina Chariots Investments
Nairobi, Kenya

Published by Mina Chariots Publishers,
A division of Mina Chariots Investments Ltd
P.O. Box 12505-00100
Nairobi
E-mail: minachariots@gmail.com

Cover illustration by John Nyaga Nyagah
Cover design by Joseph Ngari

ISBN 978-9966-1725-0-1

To my wife Anne
and children Daniel, Dominic and Peter,
for all your love and constant prodding
that makes me an insatiable seeker of the truth
and for your understanding
when I needed to keep away from you
for the many hours of silence
that made this work possible

See to it that no one takes you captive through hollow and deceptive philosophy, which depends on human tradition and the elemental spiritual forces of this world rather than on Christ.

Colossians 2:8

Contents

Introduction

In his efforts to make sense of the world around him, mankind has always tried to simplify matters by creating easily-understandable systems and theories that can be quickly grasped. The way in which one situation is solved gives a clue about how to go about similar predicaments in the future. This attempt to generalize matters for the sake of simplification is applicable in all areas of human endeavour. Every civilization through the millennia has thus sought to come to terms with challenges in its environment by coming up with customs and thought systems that seem to address its peculiar situations.

In due course, what may have initially begun as a novel reaction to an existing challenge based on the understanding of a society at a particular time degenerates into a thoughtless mannerism that everyone takes for granted. It is no longer necessarily helpful, but is done for its own sake – a lifeless custom that nobody clearly knows why they even follow it, save for some ill-defined explanation to do with "family honour," or "our fathers did it this way," or "everyone accepts this to be the truth," or some similar nebulous justification.

It is particularly tragic that such thoughtlessness has found its way into matters of faith, thanks to centuries of spiritual slumber by well-meaning Christians, turning their life-giving faith into a dead system of religion. For the sake of obscure traditions with hardly any scriptural warrant, wars have been fought, thousands have been killed and maimed, denominational splits have been explained away and millions left in spiritual bondage. Yet, Christian scholars and leaders around the world have continued to blindly support the propagation of ideologies and theological teachings that only serve to hamper the Christian witness.

Through the centuries, Christians from all walks of life have made the tragic decision to entrust their walk with God to spiritual leaders, so much that the latter's interpretation of God's word is taken to be sacrosanct; believers do not bother to find out the truth for themselves. The resulting heresies and abuse in the Body of Christ have been phenomenal.

In recent years, a good number of books have been written in an effort to restore the church to what it should be. In different ways, the authors have contributed to a fresh understanding of the church and the need to shed off many of the human traditions that have arisen in the course of two millennia of Christianity. Issues such as church buildings, the clergy-laity divide; hierarchical systems and liturgies have been exhaustively handled in different books and shown to be harmful to the gospel.

Despite this, there is a sense in which many in this new breed of Christian writers have not gone far enough. Certain traditions are still taken as sacrosanct, commanded by Christ. These include water baptism and the Lord's Supper. Taking a fresh look at the relevant texts regarding water baptism, this book argues that the practice is neither commanded nor desirable for the church. The logical consequence of this position is a rejection of all human traditions, including the Lord's Supper.

Many of the daring writers who have sought the restoration of the church have focused on returning the church to what it was in the first century. But they forget that the first century church can only be an outpost on the way, not the destination itself. We have veered so far from the path of truth over the centuries that we needed to first check out this outpost in order to recover our direction. But however commendable the efforts have been toward this goal, they are clearly insufficient: The destination we must aim for is well beyond the first century church: It is grander and more glorious. God wants the church to be restored to a higher benchmark – to that Body of Christ that the Father has always desired for His Son.

In this regard, Christians must now stop asking themselves, "What can we learn from the apostles about the church?" Rather, they must start asking, "What is the vision of the Father about the church?" We must pray for God to fill us with His vision of the Bride of the Lamb. Where the apostles in word and deed concurred with the Father's vision, then we rejoice. Whenever they deviated from the Father's vision for cultural reasons or due to their own human weaknesses, however, we have an obligation to refuse to follow their example, because our eyes are fixed not on the apostles but on Christ.

This represents a seismic shift – from focusing on a return to first-century Christianity to the kind of worship that has always existed in the mind of the Father before time began. The story of the entire bible is hinged around the restoration of all things to what God envisioned right from the beginning of creation. When "he chose us in him before the creation of the world to be holy and blameless in his sight (Ephesians 1:4)," He had a plan about how His Son would be glorified. We need to fix our eyes on that plan and vision.

In so doing, I am not advocating a departure from scripture. The Father's vision is wholly revealed in scripture. All we need to do is to elevate the Father's vision above the teaching of the early apostles. The apostolic teaching of our day, therefore, must take note of the teaching of the early church but move beyond it, because Christ is constantly at work to shed greater illumination upon His word for the sake of His church. This is not to say that today's teaching is in opposition with the early apostolic teaching, but only that as Christ sheds His light from one generation to another, issues are clarified and the church moves deeper in the direction of love.

The apostles were right in exhorting believers to love one another, but at the point where they asked slaves to obey their masters, we must deviate and show greater love by seeking freedom for any unfortunate brother or sister suffering the bondage of slavery. They were right in asking Christians to wait for one another before taking their meals, which is what any loving family ought to do; however, we know that God is not interested in Christians' obedience to a ceremony of sharing bread and wine but rather in the sharing of our lives together – which is the essence of what the apostles were doing within their own cultural set-up. When our vision is based on blindly replicating what the apostles did rather than on the Father's vision, we end up initiating bread-and-wine traditions that appear spiritual but totally miss the mark.

The churches planted by the apostles reveal much that was in agreement with the Father's vision, but also many shortcomings. The cleansing of the church to remove impurities and conform it to the Father's vision must go on until the words of John's prophetic vision are fulfilled:

> And he carried me away in the Spirit and showed me the Holy City, Jerusalem, coming down out of heaven from God. It shone with the glory of God, and its brilliance was like that of a very precious jewel, like a jasper, clear as crystal. (Revelation 21:9-11)

I am aware that the outlook I have taken represents a radically different proposition from what most believers are accustomed to, but it is my hope that the arguments outlined herein will be studied keenly and will contribute to greater enlightenment and understanding in the body of Christ, as well as the debunking of superstition. Although largely imperceptible by most believers, the propagation of spiritual-sounding but erroneous beliefs has resulted in great harm to the body of Christ through the generations. This book is one small step toward restoration of authentic faith that centres on Jesus Christ alone.

No doubt, the traditions that have arisen in Christendom over the centuries are too numerous to cover comprehensively in a book such as this one. The present work simply addresses the genesis of the sort of mind that accepts and generates traditional thinking and doctrinal errors, pointing to the importance of making a clean break from human traditions right from the beginning of the Christian walk. The spiritual walk, it is argued, must not be contaminated by seeking equivalents in physical manifestations and elements, which is the door to harmful traditions and even superstitions. Once this point has been grasped in relation to baptism, it becomes easy for the reader to apply these truths to all other human traditions and doctrines.

When people come to faith in Jesus Christ, it has been customary to take them through water baptism as an initiatory rite. They are told that this ritual – whatever the specific way in which it is practiced by a group or denomination – marks the beginning of their walk with Christ. It is therefore quite fitting that water baptism should also form the starting point of any study of human traditions in Christianity.

Isaac Mwangi
Nairobi, Kenya, December 2012

Chapter 1
The Problem with Traditions

By the time of Christ, many of the commandments and regulations codified in the Law of Moses had undergone a transformation based on the particular teachings and emphases of various groups, which included the Pharisees and the Sadducees. With time, such teachings came to supplant the original word handed down to Moses and did not consider God's intent. This is what is referred to as "the tradition of the elders" (Matt 15:2, Mk 7:3, 5).

Jesus issued a prompt rebuke for this tendency to elevate the teachings of men over the word of God. In Matthew 15:2-3, in response to the question, "Why do your disciples break the tradition of the elders? Jesus asks: "And why do you break the command of God for the sake of your tradition?"

Regardless of whatever teaching one may have become accustomed to in any area of their spiritual walk, true wisdom demands that we take nothing from fellow humans as beyond question, but rather subject everything to the scrutiny of scripture. In so doing, we must not approach the Bible as know-it-alls with the intention of seeking to prove ourselves, specific denominations or belief systems right; on the contrary, true humility requires us to ask God to speak to us. In so doing, we recognize that the beliefs we take for granted, however entrenched or widely accepted by our close circle of friends or even the general body of believers, could be based on a faulty interpretation of scripture.

Although the whole Bible is God's Word, we cannot just pick any verse at random and command obedience from Christians. We must first explore some basic issues and ask ourselves a few questions.

First, there are many voices in scripture. Whenever the devil speaks, say at the Garden of Eden or in the Book of Job, it is easy to recognize him and to ignore his advice. We are certainly not expected to imitate or obey what the devil is shown as saying in scripture.

What about the voices of men, even godly people? Shall we hate our enemies and unbelievers, for instance, because that is the example we see in David (Psalm 139:22-23)? Surely, we must be more circumspect here and approve of only what man says that at the same time agrees with what God declares. Even a good example by a godly man, say Abraham's giving of a tenth to Melchizedek, cannot be said to constitute a command for believers to do likewise unless God specifically commands this.

It might be tempting to think that when God speaks, our task is any simpler. Not so: It is critical that whenever we hear God speak in scripture, we should not rush to do the thing commanded before we ask ourselves, "Who is God speaking to?" Not everything that God says is to be obeyed literally by everyone. For instance, God instituted the covenant of circumcision with Abraham, yet most Christians will agree that circumcision is not required of them. God told Hosea to seek an adulterous wife, yet we do not advise our young men to do likewise. The examples are legion. The fact is that in these and many other instances when God speaks in the Bible, we somehow "know" that the command does not apply to ourselves.

This means we must seek to understand the whole context in which a command is given in its plain meaning, without spiritualizing it. When anyone picks out a few words or verses out of context and proceeds to create a whole theology from there, that person is clearly being selfish and not faithful to scripture – however noble the intentions.

An often ignored aspect of interpretation is a consideration of what any part of Scripture means in the Spirit as against the letter. This does not have to take us into the world of superstition or conjecture. To determine what a phrase or verse means in the Spirit is simply to consider the context in which words are spoken or written and put this against the backdrop of the whole teaching of scripture.

As a quick example, Paul exhorts the Corinthians to give generously (2 Corinthians 9:6-7), and a lot of abuse has resulted from not putting these words into context. From the context, we see that Paul spoke these words in relation to helping the poor victims of a famine in Jerusalem. When we use Paul's words in order to benefit others, particularly people in distress, we are fully in the Spirit. However, when these words are applied to raise funds to enrich preachers or put up imposing cathedrals, we use the letter but fail to grasp the Spirit. The Spirit has to do with being faithful to the intent expressed in the context. And the intent of the Spirit in New Testament giving is always about showing love to others, particularly the vulnerable in society; this sort of giving is never for the purpose of putting up beautiful buildings, paying salaries to preachers or buying flashy cars and designer suits for them.

Unfortunately, legalisms are created from this failure to get to the intent of the Spirit. Starting at the very beginning of the Christian life with baptism, human traditions – whether from precedents in the bible or stemming from extra-biblical sources – arise out of human failure to grasp the message of the Spirit.

This is particularly due to an inability to comprehend abstract truths. This weakness, in turn, leads to ridiculous practices and traditions when matters are brought from the spiritual realm and applied directly into the physical world. If this were not so, baptism would never involve water; the Lord's Supper would not be about food and drink; church would have nothing to do with special buildings; and the priesthood would not be a reference to a special class of believers in a hierarchical organization.

When we focus on physical elements rather than spiritual reality, we show that we are still dwelling in the religion of copies and shadows; it means we have not comprehended the superior nature of our calling in Christ. The writer to the Hebrews put the matter thus to his readers:

> Every high priest is appointed to offer both gifts and sacrifices, and so it was necessary for this one also to have something to offer. If he were on earth, he would not be a priest, for there are already priests who offer the gifts prescribed by the law. They serve at a sanctuary that is a copy and shadow of what is in heaven. This is why Moses was warned when he was about to build the tabernacle: "See to it that you make everything according to the pattern shown you on the mountain." But in fact the ministry Jesus has received is as superior to theirs as the covenant of which he is mediator is superior to the old one, since the new covenant is established on better promises. (Hebrews 8:3-6)

Although the writer to the Hebrews was referring to the worship at the Jerusalem temple being a shadow of what takes place in heaven, what the church has done through the ages is to substitute new external forms for the heavenly worship. Although the church may claim to no longer offer animal sacrifices, yet these other external forms are no more acceptable to Christian worship than Mosaic practices would be. We nullify the work of Jesus at the cross in bringing about the end of the law when we create even more rituals and regulations. Paul's words to the Galatians ring true to this day:

> "I do not set aside the grace of God, for if righteousness could be gained through the law, Christ died for nothing!" (Galatians 2:21)

In the New Testament, the apostles provide a wonderful context of interpreting the Christian life. Ignorantly following what they did without seeking the counsel of the Spirit, however, has only resulted in more legalisms. Just as in the Old Testament examples of Abraham and David, we are supposed to be discerning. Where the apostles deviated from the clear voice of the Lord, we are obviously not expected to follow their example and similarly go into error. The word of God clearly exhorts us to fix our eyes on Jesus (Hebrews 12:1). Where the apostles erred, it would be expected of us to take note of that error as a lesson to ourselves.

I submit that this attitude glorifies God more than a stand that elevates the apostles above any kind of error, even in the practice of their faith, and that obligates believers to try and do everything exactly as the apostles may have done it. We must be discerning to know what to hold on to and what to give up. In the tenets of the faith and Christ-centred beliefs and practices, we must stand to be counted with the apostles. In terms of social customs that affected the practice of the apostles' faith, we must realize that we belong to vastly different socio-cultural situations. And where the apostles, for purely human reasons, may have faltered in the exercise of their faith, we would be foolish to follow their example.

As more and more traditions are piled onto the believer, they worsen the emasculation of the body of Christ, individually and corporately. They help create carnal Christians who remain spiritual babies throughout their lives. They lead believers to focus on outward forms, symbols, sacred days and ceremonies that are of no value rather than on an inner peace with God. They contribute to mind control and exploitation of gullible believers. They foment church splits and disputes over non-issues. Worst of all, they remove the Christian's and church's focus from Christ, who should always be at the centre for us all to behold his glory.

Such results could only be produced by an evil genius. Human traditions are not to the glory of God: These are practices that must be confronted honestly and wholesale rather than piecemeal.

Chapter 2
Only one baptism

As an initiation rite, water baptism is widely accepted and practiced in many Christian groups and denominations around the world. While there are certainly differences in the way it is administered, there is little debate regarding its central role to mark the beginning of a believer's walk with Christ.

The issues that have divided Christians in the practice of baptism are legion. Should it be administered to children or is it purely a believers' baptism? Is it essential for salvation? Who should administer it? What formula should be used: (a) in the name of the Father, the Son and the Holy Spirit or (b) in the name of Jesus Christ? Is it to be done by immersion or sprinkling? Can a different element be used as a substitute for water?

There is also what some believers call the "baptism of the Holy Spirit", or in the Holy Spirit, or by the Holy Spirit, the description largely depending on whatever sectarian perspective is taught. How does this sort of baptism relate with water baptism? Some denominations teach a two-stage approach, whereby a believer is first baptized using the element of water, after which he is expected to experience the Holy Spirit baptism sometime thereafter.

Scholars have debated around these and related issues for

centuries. Rarely, however, has the issue been fundamentally examined: Does scripture really sanction the ritual of water baptism?

Whenever we see a teaching bringing so much strife and division, it behooves us to look more closely at that teaching and to ask ourselves searching questions. Surely, if something is of such fundamental importance as to command universal obedience in the manner that water baptism is said to do, God would be quite clear about it in scripture. Why would the Lord want to leave His church to expend so much energy and go through all the heartache that's been there over the past two millennia over such a basic command, if really He has willed the practice?

Again, going by Jesus' words that only "a bad tree bears bad fruit," (Matthew 7:17), how possible is it that a practice commanded by a good and loving God would result in so much strife and division? That in itself should ring the alarm bells in our spiritual antennae.

With the diversity of opinions in Christendom, it is easy to despair and assume that it is impossible to know the truth. Or perhaps the temptation may come to take the stand that it really doesn't matter and that all baptisms are valid. As John Calvin stated:

> But whether the person being baptized should be wholly immersed, and whether thrice or once, whether he should only be sprinkled with poured water – these details are of no importance, but ought to be optional to churches according to the diversity of countries. Yet the word 'baptize' means to immerse, and it is clear that the rite of immersion was observed in the ancient church. (John Calvin, *Institutes of the Christian Religion,* Vol. 4 Chapter 15 section 19, p599).

Where the bible is not indifferent, however, man has absolutely no authority to grant himself that licence. Every Christian who takes his or her faith seriously does not want to cultivate the attitude that God doesn't care about whatever beliefs and practices we encourage. The bible is clear that these myriad baptisms cannot possibly be all correct, for only one can be valid:

> There is one body and one Spirit, just as you were called to one hope when you were called; one Lord, one faith, one baptism; one God and Father of all, who is over all and through all and in all. (Ephesians 4:4-6)

Since the word of God here declares that there is only ONE BAPTISM, it is our task as followers of Jesus to find out what this true baptism is and to adhere to that one baptism only. God cannot be the author of confusion.

A laissez faire attitude in the interpretation of the word of God has led to much confusion in many areas of Christian life. In our prayer life, our understanding of what the blood of Jesus does, the Lord's Supper, the church, giving, the Christian priesthood and many other areas, we have allowed this anything-goes attitude to dominate. The truth, rather than being from God as revealed in His word, becomes a relative reality that is dependent on ourselves and can be changed to suit our whims and desires. Those who stand for the truth of the gospel will no doubt find such a situation unacceptable. If we are to cultivate an attitude of reverential obedience to God's word, we must inculcate that frame of mind in every area of the believer's walk, right from baptism. But which baptism, for only one can be true?

Chapter 3
Hangovers from the Old Testament

Intertwined with the myriad ceremonies and rituals described in the Law of Moses in the Old Testament, we find references to certain washings. In Leviticus 8:6 we read: "Then Moses brought Aaron and his sons forward and washed them with water." This line occurs in a passage that describes the ordination of Aaron and his sons. Other aspects of this ordination included garments, anointing oil, a sin offering and a burnt offering, all described in detail.

In the book of Numbers, we find the Lord separating for Himself the Levites from other Israelites. He commands Moses:

> To purify them, do this: Sprinkle the water of cleansing on them; then have them shave their whole bodies and wash their clothes. And so they will purify themselves. (Numbers 8:7)

Apart from such consecrations, washings were also commanded on other occasions. One of these was upon contact with a mold in a house, Leviticus 14:47: "Anyone who sleeps or eats in the house will be unclean till evening."

Yet another occasion requiring ritual washing with water involved all sorts of discharges by both men and women:

Whoever touches the man who has a discharge must wash their clothes and bathe with water, and they will be unclean till evening. If the man with the discharge spits on anyone who is clean, they must wash their clothes and bathe with water, and they will be unclean till evening. (Leviticus 15:7-8)

Emission of semen was not excluded from such rules either:

When a man has an emission of semen, he must bathe his whole body with water, and it will be unclean till evening. Any clothing or leather that has semen on it must be washed with water, and it will be unclean till evening. When a man has sexual relations with a woman and there is an emission of semen, both of them must bathe with water, and they will be unclean till evening. (Leviticus 15:16-18)

A discharge by a woman from menstrual discharge or any irregular flow of blood was also included among these regulations:

"Any bed she lies on while her discharge continues will be unclean, as is her bed during her monthly period, and anything she sits on will be unclean, as during her period. Anyone who touches them will be unclean; they must wash their clothes and bathe with water, and they will be unclean till evening. (Leviticus 15:26-27)

With this background, it is much easier for us to understand that when King David saw Bathsheba bathing, she was evidently purifying herself (2 Samuel: 11:2-4) in obedience to what was commanded in the Law of Moses.

Abolition of the Law of Moses

Apart from ritual baths – which by the time of Jesus had evolved into baptisms – there are many other practices found in the New Testament period that have their origins in the Old Testament.

The New Testament declares that the Law was but a shadow, the reality being found in Christ Himself (Colossians 2:17, Hebrews 10:1). Jesus Himself repeatedly said that the Law and the Prophets spoke about Him, which scriptures He had come to fulfill. He says He did not come to abolish the Law or the Prophets (Matthew 5:17), but neither does He say – as many people wrongly interpret – that He had come to strengthen or to perpetuate the Law. He came merely to accomplish what had been foreshadowed by the Law and prophesied in the past. Once that had been achieved, the whole Law stood abolished at the cross.

The New Testament is quite clear about the Law having reached an end with the coming of the new dispensation. As far as non-Jews were concerned, the apostles were very clear following the controversy that necessitated the Council at Jerusalem (Acts 15) that the Gentiles were not to be bound by the Law of Moses, but would in love abstain from those things that would give offense to their Jewish brothers and thus hinder fellowship with them.

Some of these things were not necessarily sinful, such as eating particular foodstuffs (Christ had declared all foods clean in Mark 7:19, with Paul also declaring that the kingdom of God is not about eating and drinking in Romans 14:17, among other texts). However, the exercise of this freedom by the Gentiles would have created problems with the Jews, who for centuries had been forbidden from eating those foodstuffs by the Law and considered them disgusting:

For the law of Moses has been preached in every city form the earliest times and is read in the synagogues on every Sabbath. (Acts 15:21)

But even for those Jews who could overcome the hangovers of their past adherence to the Law, nothing was to prevent them from enjoying their freedom in Christ:

But now, by dying to what once bound us, we have been released from the law so that we serve in the new way of the Spirit, and not in the old way of the written code. (Romans 7:6)

Indeed, the Law had served to create enmity between Jews and Gentiles by lifting up the former as God's chosen people, who then looked down upon other nations. Part of the work that Christ achieved at Calvary was to demolish this invisible wall that existed between the two groups:

For He Himself is our peace, who made both groups into one, and broke down the barrier of the dividing wall, by abolishing in his flesh the enmity, which is the law of commandments contained in ordinances, that in Himself He might make the two into one new man, thus establishing peace, and might reconcile them both in one body to God through the cross, by it having put to death the enmity. (Ephesians 2: 14-16, NASB)

If, after a careful reading of these and other New Testament texts concerning the abolition of the law at the cross, there is still any doubt in anyone's mind that indeed the law has been completely and finally abolished, the writer to the Hebrews does not mince his words:

The former regulation is set aside because it was weak and useless (for the law made nothing perfect), and a better hope is introduced, by which we draw near to God. (Hebrews 7:18-19)

Writing about the ministry of the priests appointed according to the law to perform various tasks and offer sacrifices, the same writer says:

But in fact the ministry Jesus has received is as superior to theirs as the covenant of which he is mediator is superior to the old one, since the new covenant is established on better promises.
For if there had been nothing wrong with that first covenant, no place would have been sought for another. (Hebrews 8:6-7)

Concerning the rituals and sacrifices offered by the temple priests, and in particular the restriction that the High Priest alone could enter the Most Holy Place and that only once a year, the writer to the Hebrews says:

The Holy Spirit was showing by this that the way into the Most Holy Place had not yet been disclosed as long as the first tabernacle was still functioning. This is an illustration for the present time, indicating that the gifts and sacrifices being offered were not able to clear the conscience of the worshipper. They are only a matter of food and drink and various ceremonial washings – external regulations applying until the time of the new order. (Hebrews 9:8-10)

If these regulations applied until the time of the new order – which most Christians agree began at Calvary – then the continued observance of any of the Old Testament ordinances can only be explained as a hangover from the past borne of an inability to let go of a deeply ingrained worldview. And since it has been demonstrated that water baptism among Jews in the New Testament period was a continuation of the ceremonial washings of the Old Testament, this ritual falls under the ambit of the "external regulations applying until the time of the new order." This new order having come into effect at the cross, water baptism has no place in the lives of believers. In this, it joins pilgrimages, animal sacrifices, anointing with oil, tithes and all those rituals and regulations recorded in the books of the law as an external regulation that is of absolutely no value to New Covenant believers.

When we read of any apostle or other follower of Jesus recorded in the pages of the bible as teaching or practicing any such outward forms, it ought to be a lesson to us about the difficulty of turning people from the rigid stranglehold of traditions, but not an example for Christians to follow blindly and perpetuate such errors.

People will often ask, "Why then do we need to read the Old Testament?" Well, the main answer to this question is that we need to understand the history of our salvation. By reading the Old Testament, we get to know about the Fall and why it was necessary for Jesus to come. God's work in preparing the way for the coming of our Saviour is revealed through types and shadows, that it may be easier for those who are chosen to inherit salvation to understand the fulfillment that took place when Christ came. We do not read history lessons in order to replicate the lifestyles of people who lived a thousand years ago; neither should we study the Old Testament and find therein a justification to start practising polygamy, circumcising our children at the age of eight days, performing animal sacrifices, undertaking ritual washings or seeking tithes.

Judaic influences in Christianity

When it comes to the Mosaic Code, the New Testament makes it clear that this does not apply to New Covenant believers. If it can be shown that a practice is based on the teachings of the Law of Moses or indeed any other Old Testament commands, then that practice cannot be made binding on the New Testament people of God. While the Old Testament is largely preoccupied with external forms and regulations, the testament initiated by Jesus Christ at the cross is all about inner transformation and peace with God. To insist on external forms as a means of grace is to miss the essence of the New Testament.

The attitude of following apostolic practices blindly removes our focus from Christ and places it on humans. But the word of God never tells us to do this, regardless of how great or godly or inspirational we may find a particular person to be. Indeed, the apostles themselves consistently asked believers to focus on Christ. In Philippians 2:5, Paul writes, "In your relationships with one another, have the same attitude of mind Christ Jesus had." The writer to the Hebrews says it even more clearly, telling believers to "fix your thoughts on Jesus" (Hebrews 3:1) and later, "Let us fix our eyes on Jesus, the author and perfecter of our faith." (Hebrews 12:2, NIV).

Certainly, the apostles would have been loath to ask Christians to remove their focus from Christ and place it on themselves. Indeed, Paul had occasion to rebuke those who had started doing so in Corinth by declaring their preferred allegiances to Paul, Apollos or Peter (1 Corinthians 1:12).

While no doubt we should study how the apostles lived out their faith and learn from them, believers are under no obligation to outwardly practice their faith exactly as the apostles did. While at the core we are to follow their example of Christ-centredness and simplicity in living out our faith, it would be foolish to copy even the cultural aspects in which they lived.

Moreover, every believer who declares they are following the example of the apostles in performing a rite engages in selective obedience. Going through the New Testament, one will find many other rites that they simply brush over. It should be understood that being only human and particularly because they still operated within their own cultural context, the early Jewish believers were unable to completely let go of their previous way of life in Judaism.

This explains why the apostles observed hours of prayer. In Acts 3:1, Luke says, "Peter and John were going up to the temple at the time of prayer – at three in the afternoon." Now, how many Christians feel obliged to set 3:00pm as their time of prayer in adherence to this "apostolic practice"? Or for those converted from other faiths, to visit their former places of worship for prayer?

Clearly, the apostles still went to synagogues and to the temple – though this was partly for evangelizing purposes. However, to their credit, they clearly understood that the new people of God were not called upon to erect houses of worship, and none was built by them.

At the beginning of Acts 16, Paul meets Timothy and circumcises him before embarking with him on his journey. Do we feel obliged by what this apostle did to command the circumcision of all who come to Christ? Why not?

Even James could not overcome this weakness, urging anyone who was sick to be anointed with oil by elders, who would pray for him. But why not just have prayer without any application of a physical element? Does oil, or water, or any other physical element aid in God's power to bring about healing? Of course, the answer to this is a definite no. The injunction to use oil, then, emanated from James's Jewish past rather than any requirement of the new faith in Jesus Christ. With this understanding, we can comfortably ignore the use of oil and rebuke preachers who steal from the sheep by selling oil to them. Our money is better spent buying medicine for the sick.

Because the transition from the Old Testament regulations to freedom in Christ could not have been achieved overnight given this human tendency to hold on to the past, it is understandable that there are so many Judaic hangovers in the pages of the New Testament. This also explains the constant friction that existed between the slow learners and the reformers, principally Paul.

In a move to appease the Jews, Paul at one point agreed to go through Jewish purification rites, but even this did not help matters and there was a near-riot in Jerusalem:

When the seven days were nearly over, some Jews from the province of Asia saw Paul at the temple. They stirred up the whole crowd and seized him, shouting, "People of Israel, help us! This is the man who teaches everyone everywhere against our people and our law and this place. And besides, he has brought Greeks into the temple and defiled this holy place." (Acts 21:27-28)

While many people will not feel obliged to replicate all the apostles' actions and observe 3:00pm as the time of prayer, or engage in purification rites, or insist on the circumcision of new converts, for some strange reason they quote apostolic practice when it comes to baptism.

However, from the foregoing discussion, it should be quite obvious that whenever we come across Jewish practices in the New Testament, we should be very circumspect before assuming that this is a normative obligation for every Christian. In some instances, as in Paul's situation in Jerusalem, he was simply giving in to the Jews because of the pressure on him and possibly for his own safety. We would be foolish to start observing purification rites simply because an apostle of Paul's standing did that.

Where Jewish rituals were not done as a result of such direct pressure, then this can be explained as a hangover from the past, not because scripture demands such observance. These rituals would have included ceremonial washings – read water baptism – which the writer to the Hebrews includes among those practices that applied until the time of the new order.

Now that the new order has arrived, the ceremonial washing we commonly call water baptism is no longer commanded or even desired for God's people to perform. Just like tithes, first fruits, pilgrimages and all the other regulations of the Old Covenant, it's time ended at the cross.

Indeed, water baptism and other external forms that still hold pride of place among Christians are evidence of the carnality of many believers around the world. For while scripture says, "We live (or walk) by faith, not by sight," many of them go about their Christian lives in a manner that suggests the reverse.

Scripture says believers are the temple of the Holy Spirit, yet they will not be content without replicating Solomon's feat of impressive physical temples that their eyes can see; Jesus says He will be with them wherever two or three are gathered in His name, yet they still imagine Christ cares more about huge multitudes; God says He speaks through the small, still voice, but they imagine that powerful orators and performers hold the secret to hearing God's word clearly; they are told the curtain was torn in two and all may approach the throne of grace, but they still place themselves under a clergy that then installs itself as a mediator between God and man; although God says He has anointed them, they still seek physical oil; and every time they read about being baptized into Christ, water comes into mind.

Thus they turn every spiritual reality into an opportunity to indulge the flesh.

Chapter 4
Futile reforms

Through the centuries, men of noble intention have sought to formulate a clear biblical teaching on baptism and to unify Christianity on this matter. These efforts have largely been futile.

According to Frank Viola, "Most of what we do for 'church' was lifted directly out of pagan culture in the post-apostolic period." (*Pagan Christianity*, p27-28). Although water baptism had its origins in apostolic practice, he says, pagan influences led to the numerous disagreements that subsequently came to the fore regarding the details of actual practice.

Tertullian (c160-225) wrote his treatise *On Baptism* to counter Gnostic practices, particularly the baptismal rite practiced by a woman of a Gnostic sect. According to Tertullian, "They who are about to enter baptism ought to pray with repeated prayers, fasts, and bendings of the knee, and vigils all the night through, and with the confession of all by-gone sins." The best time for conducting the rite, he says, is during the Passover.

His treatise also opposed the baptism of infants. Despite this opposition to the baptism of babies and young children from those early days, the debate has continued through the centuries. As one record has put it:

Such matters still deeply divide Christians today, and disputes about the appropriate understanding of New Testament texts relating to baptism are unlikely to disappear. Whatever is to be said on the various sides of these debates, the reality is that neither an argument in favour of baptizing babies today nor an argument against the practice can be established conclusively on the grounds of historical evidence about the earliest customs of the churches. It is clear that in the late second and early third centuries infants were being baptized in at least a number of contexts and that a system of adults acting as sponsors was already in operation in these places. (John D. Woodbridge and David F. Wright (eds), The Monarch History of the Church, Volume 1, *The Birth of the Church*, p 279).

During the time of Augustine, the Donatist Church was more popular in North Africa than the Catholic Church. The Donatists believed that the baptisms conducted by the Catholic Church were powerless because of the moral laxity of its priests. This forced Augustine to come up with a new concept: That the worth of a sacrament has nothing to do with the moral condition of the priest who administers it. He argued that, "When Peter baptizes, it is Christ who baptizes. When Paul baptizes, it is Christ who baptizes. When Judas baptizes, it is Christ who baptizes." (Jonathan Hill, *The History of Christian Thought,* p86).

It never occurred to Augustine, so it seems, that Christ does not in that case need a human activity to prompt him to accept union with a believer. The irony of a union with Christ that required sanctioning by Judas in order to be counted as valid never struck him.

But Augustine went even further in perpetrating some of the false doctrines that have held millions in bondage to this day. He taught that baptism is an essential precondition for salvation. Babies who die before baptism cannot be saved. He also suggested that there exist different degrees of punishment in hell and that unbaptized infants suffer only lightly. (Jonathan Hill, p91).

In recent times, too, various leaders both in the denominational and house church movements have come up with suggested reforms. Neil Cole has called for greater participation in baptism by the body of Christ:

> Christians are actually instructed to disobey Jesus when they are told not to baptize their disciples. The practice of baptism is not something Christ gave to the church organization but to all disciples. One of the sayings in our own church-planting movement is "The bible doesn't command us to be baptized but to be baptizers." There is absolutely no biblical support for the idea that only the clergy in the local church can baptize. Though our traditions and experience may reinforce these standards, the Bible does not.
>
> It is amazing how much damage the simple idea of baptizing another has caused through church history. People have been killed, cults have been initiated, denominations started and split, heretics burned at the stake, and parachurch organizations have been formed – all because we view baptism in a strange, unbiblical fashion. If we would only view the Bible and take it for what it says literally, rather than defend our "sacred" traditions, the church would be healthier. (Neil Cole, *Organic Leadership: Leading naturally right where you are*, p110.)

The new ground broken is therefore the wider participation in this rite by the body of Christ – not a questioning of the authenticity of this practice. It is taken for granted that indeed baptism is commanded in the Great Commission. But how could something be so beneficial and commanded by Christ yet lead to murders, cults and division? Doesn't this fruit justify a re-examination of the whole question of baptism to "unmask" it? If the fruit is bad, a re-examination of the whole tree of baptism is certainly in order.

In his excellent work on the emergence of unscriptural traditions in the church, *Pagan Christianity*, Frank Viola writes in support of believers' baptism as opposed to infant baptism. He also takes a stand for immersion as against sprinkling. In his opinion, the New Testament is in support of both of these positions. He also advocates baptism immediately following conversion:

> However, it is typical in most modern churches for baptism to be separated from conversion by great lengths of time. Many Christians were saved at one age and baptized at a much later age. In the first century, this was unheard of... Water baptism was the outward confession of a person's faith. But more than that, it was the way someone came to the Lord in Century One. For this reason, the confession of baptism is vitally linked to the exercise of saving faith. So much so that the NT writers often use "baptism" in place of the word "faith" and link it to being "saved." This is because baptism was the early Christian's confession of faith in Christ." (*Pagan Christianity,* pp 234-5)

While logically well-reasoned and – on the face of it – consistent with the New Testament, Frank's reasons in support of a "reformed" baptism fail on at least two grounds. First of all, baptism was not the way people came to the Lord – not in the first century and not today. People have always come to the Lord through faith in Jesus Christ. The thief on the cross did come to the Lord without water baptism. Secondly, in the Acts of the Apostles, the Lord's clear calling is often spelt out and preceded water baptism, which was done as a custom but never as a clear command from God. The two – God's calling and water baptism – are no doubt wholly separated.

This means that where we see some mix-up in that water baptism is often used in place of "faith," as Frank points out, the answer lies in the confusion existing in the minds of believers at that time. This is not to doubt the inspiration of the whole of the New Testament. No, all what it means is that we need to understand the historical context or worldview of the writer of those words.

Interpretation of the Word, rather than taking the "letter", is something that we constantly do, whether consciously or unconsciously. We who have the benefit of reading the whole Scripture have no excuse for taking the "letter" and forcing women to wear headscarves and to remain silent in church; or insisting believers must be anointed with oil; or initiating a weekly ritual of unleavened bread and wine. If any of these sounds awkward, then neither should we decree that all believers must be baptized in water. Such actions only show that we have fallen short of the Spirit. Well, we could as well insist baptism must be done in the river Jordan! Or that we must greet one another with holy kisses, on top of making a collection for the Jerusalem church every Sunday.

An assumption related to this and that has bound many Christians but now needs to be debunked is the implied hermeneutic that all what the apostles did constitutes a normative command for all Christians at all times. This is obviously true in terms of the way they gathered under the headship of Christ, conducted themselves in humility without titles and offices, boldly evangelized the world around them, remained firm in their faith in the face of persecution and suffering, and showed love to one another.

But this is not the case when we come to non-essential, customary habits and Judaic customs; where these appear to take pride of place alongside essential Christian teachings, we must have the wisdom to sieve them out. Such customs include adherence to hours of prayer (Acts 3:1); circumcision (Acts 16:3); vows and purification rites (Acts 21:22-24); anointing with oil (James 5:14) and of course baptism. Even the Sunday collection is not mandatory for Christians dwelling under the freedom of the Spirit; after the cross, nothing must be allowed to become a legalism cast in stone.

Chapter 5
What's in a name?

◦───❀❀───◦

One of the major arguments to erupt within evangelical Christianity has revolved around the formula of the words that should be spoken by the baptizer during water baptism.

One school of thought has maintained that the proper formula should be, "In the name of Jesus Christ." Another has advocated the more traditional rendering, "In the name of the Father and of the Son and of the Holy Spirit."

Traditional view

Those who support the traditional form draw their support from Jesus' words contained in what is commonly referred to as the Great Commission:

> Then Jesus came to them and said, "All authority in heaven and on earth has been given to me. Therefore go and make disciples of all nations, baptizing them in the name of the Father and of the Son and of the Holy Spirit, and teaching them to obey everything I have commanded you. And surely I am with you always, to the very end of the age." (Matthew 28:18-20)

These words are taken as a command from the Lord not only

to put people through the ritual of water baptism, but also to do so while reciting a specific formula. After reading Chapter 7, it will be clear why this text cannot possibly be commanding a formula for baptism. For now, however, let us remember the words of Paul in 2 Corinthians 3: "The letter kills, but the Spirit gives life." Our actions as Christians ought not to be determined by what the letter says, even where it appears the bible or even the New Testament in particular expressly commands something. We must always find out what the mind of the Spirit is by seeking the whole counsel of scripture on an issue as well as examining the context – cultural, historical and otherwise – in which a command is given.

This should not be as difficult to fathom as it may initially appear. In Ephesians 6:5 we come across this command:

Slaves, obey your earthly masters with respect and fear, and with sincerity of heart, just as you would obey Christ. (Ephesians 6:5)

But not many Christians give this verse the same weight as this other command just a few lines earlier:

Children, obey your parents in the Lord, for this is right. (Ephesians 6:1)

The question is, Why do we give weight to one verse and neglect the other? Many Christians certainly – and correctly – find the very thought of entertaining slavery abhorrent and would be ready to fight the practice through all possible means. The royal law of love, taken to its logical conclusion, does not allow for enslavement of our fellow men and women.

Or take the injunction against eating blood in Acts 15:20 and 29. How many of us really care about food laws? Many

Christians properly understand that the injunctions placed here against Gentile Christians were simply for the purpose of ensuring that fellowship is not hindered between Gentile and Jewish Christians since the latter found certain foods repulsive – the result of centuries of teaching in the law of Moses. We are to similarly give up in love anything that may stand in the way of fellowship with other brethren – including, of course, foodstuffs that may be unacceptable to people in cultures that we interact with. The letter, then, commands avoidance of certain foods; the Spirit, however, shows us that this is not really about food but fellowship in love.

Perhaps even more compelling is a comparison of the command to baptize in the Great Commission with other commands that were also given by Jesus but that we choose to overlook. For instance, in John 13 Jesus washes his disciples' feet, after which he gives them a very definite and authoritative command that is even clearer than the command to baptize:

Now that I, your Lord and Teacher, have washed your feet, you also should wash one another's feet. I have set you an example that you should do as I have done for you. Very truly I tell you, servants are not greater than their master, nor are messengers greater than the one who sent them. Now that you know these things, you will be blessed if you do them. (John 13:14-17)

Only a few denominations within Christianity take the command to wash one another's feet literally and practice it regularly. Of course, no believer has the sanction to teach and practice a command in Matthew 28 while ignoring an even clearer command in John 13. So, why the double standards? Some may want to suggest that washing feet was an example from our Lord regarding the kind of love that his followers should have, but not a legalism that Christ established. As Wayne Grudem puts it:

"While all Christians would profit from pondering the application of Jesus' statement about footwashing to their present patterns of life, none should think that Jesus is encouraging them to practice a ceremony of footwashing." (Wayne Grudem, *Systematic Theology: An introduction to biblical doctrine*, 1994, p962)

Excellent argument: This shows an advancement in understanding from the letter and into the Spirit. The question is: Why not do this for the whole Scripture and not just selective portions according to our whims?

Why not use this interpretive method for the Lord's command to eat bread and drink wine in his memory, as commanded in 1 Corinthians 11:23-25? Why not also apply the same standard to the command to baptize in Matthew 28:18-20? What good reason is there for holding double standards by saying footwashing was not commanded as a physical ritual while at the same time insisting that the Lord's Supper and baptism are to be observed as rituals? Very likely, such a hermeneutic is based on man's convenience and comfort; we don't want to deal with smelly socks and so we find a way of going about that even as we retain other less inconveniencing rituals.

If baptism is truly commanded as a physical ritual, we must see this in the Spirit, not just the letter. This aspect is examined more fully in Chapter 7.

Baptism in the name of Jesus

Soon after I began my walk in organic church life, I attended a meeting of a restorationist group near Nairobi where some of the Christians present argued strongly that the only true baptism was that which had been conducted "in the name of Jesus Christ." Any other baptism, they confidently said, consisted merely in "taking a bath."

It almost sounds magical. Merely changing the formula from "In the name of the Father…" to "In the name of Jesus Christ" makes the difference between a bath and true baptism! Mere human words, so to speak, determine what is acceptable and what is not acceptable before God. It is a testimony of the demonic trap the church has sunk into that such a meaningless debate should preoccupy the minds of eminent bible scholars and preachers around the world.

But let us first examine the reasons advanced by advocates of water baptism using the formula, "In the name of Jesus Christ." First and foremost is the practice of the apostles. It will be quickly pointed out by those who support this formula that the apostles, being interpreters of the gospels, baptized believers using the formula, "In the name of Jesus Christ" or variants of this. In Acts 2:38, the apostle Peter tells his hearers to "Repent and be baptized, every one of you, in the name of Jesus Christ for the forgiveness of sins." The same Peter, after preaching to the household of Cornelius and witnessing the Holy Spirit coming down upon the gathering, "ordered that they be baptized in the name of Jesus Christ." (Acts 10:48)

But it wasn't just Peter who did this. When Paul met a group of people in Ephesus who had only undergone the baptism of John, he told them about Jesus, following which "they were baptized into the name of the Lord Jesus." (Acts 19:5) Even the believers in Samaria are said to have "simply been baptized into the name of the Lord Jesus." (Acts 8:16)

Thus, proponents of this position will quickly and with scriptural evidence point out that in every instance where a name is mentioned in relation to baptism, it is the name of Jesus Christ or its variants, never "the name of the Father and of the Son and of the Holy Spirit." And because these groups tend to deny the Trinity, they will explain the latter formula as a description of God's name: To them, "the Father and the Son and the Holy Spirit" simply describes Jesus Christ. But because Christians know Him better, they refer to Him by His proper name and are baptized into the name of Jesus Christ, as did the apostles. A compelling argument indeed, or is it?

The important question to ask ourselves in relation to this position is this: Do the words, "In the name of Jesus Christ" denote a formula? To answer this question satisfactorily, we need to look at other instances in the New Testament where these words have been used, not just in relation to baptism.

In Colossians 3:17, Paul exhorts the believers: "And whatever you do, whether in word or deed, do it all in the name of the Lord Jesus, giving thanks to God the Father through him." He surely could not have meant that our every sentence ("in word") must be punctuated by the words "in the name of the Lord Jesus." It is obvious too that he could hardly have meant that every action – sitting, standing, reading, walking, eating, whatever ("in deed") – must also be interspersed with a proclamation of these words.

Such an injunction would be practically impossible for anyone to fulfill, leave alone being highly legalistic. Paul must certainly have been referring to an inner disposition, an attitude of the heart to submit to the will of the Lord in all our words and actions. It is not about a formula; it is all about Jesus' authority.

This meaning comes out clearly when we examine the events following the healing of the cripple at the Temple narrated in Acts 3. When Peter and John were brought before the Sanhedrin,

WHAT'S IN A NAME?

they were asked: "By what power or what name did you do this?" (Acts 4:7) The questioners could hardly have been interested in a formula; they wanted to know by what power, or authority, the healing had been done. In response, Peter told them: "It is by the name of Jesus Christ of Nazareth, whom you crucified but whom God raised from the dead, that this man stands before you healed." Peter was referring to the power and authority of Jesus, not some magic formula.

Indeed, at the conclusion of the session of the Sanhedrin, the latter called in Peter and John again, "and commanded them not to speak or teach at all in the name of Jesus." (Acts 4:17-18) I believe it would have meant little to the Sanhedrin if the apostles had decided to alter their terminology and preach about "the Messiah" or about "the name of Christ" rather than "the name of Jesus." They could not have been prohibiting a formula: They were essentially attempting to bring down the whole movement that derives its authority from Jesus. This is the way the apostles understood it and firmly stood their ground against their accusers, asking God to continue "to heal and perform signs and wonders through the name of your holy servant Jesus." (Acts 4:30)

Clearly, then, to act or do something "in the name of" does not necessarily refer to a formula. Even in everyday life, a lawyer acts in the name of a client, who has given the lawyer authority to act on his behalf. One who acts in the name of another has been given a trust to do so. And whether such a person mentions the words that he or she is acting "in the name of" so-and-so or does not bother to do so since this may already be well known by those concerned, it is the authority that counts.

That real authority is more important than mere words can be demonstrated from scripture by looking at the incident involving the sons of Sceva:

49

Some Jews who went around driving out evil spirits tried to invoke the name of the Lord Jesus over those who were demon-possessed. They would say, "In the name of the Jesus whom Paul preaches, I command you to come out." Seven sons of Sceva, a Jewish chief priest, were doing this. One day, the evil spirit answered them, "Jesus I know, and I know about Paul, but who are you?" Then the man who had the evil spirit jumped on them and overpowered them all. He gave them such a beating that they ran out of the house naked and bleeding. (Acts 19:13-16)

If the formula "In the name of Jesus" was sufficient in spiritual matters, things would not have gone terribly awry for the sons of Sceva. They tried to cast out demons that way, but they lacked authority from Christ. No wonder so many "Christians" have undergone all the right rituals and formulas that they can imagine, yet sadly they have been given such a beating by the enemy that their homes, churches and lifestyles are all in bad shape.

God by His grace can still perform miracles even among those who use formulas and legalisms, but what really matters is authority through unity with Christ. The debate should not be about whether we should use the formula "In the name of the Father..." or "In the name of Jesus Christ." Such a discussion only distracts from the business of empowering God's people. A formula simply encourages superstitious thinking. Why use any at all?

Chapter 6
The evidence of the gospels

L ike many other Mosaic rules that underwent modification with time, we find that by the time of the New Testament period, the washings mentioned in the Law have evolved into baptisms. This included the baptism of John, which involved immersion into the river Jordan. Apparently, there were also baptisms taking place among Gentile communities, hence there were people being "baptized for the dead" in Corinth (1 Corinthians 15:29).

That the baptism of John is closely linked to the ceremonial washings in the Old Testament can be discerned from a reading of John 3:22-26. The context in this passage is baptism. In the middle of this passage, however, we read:

> An argument developed between some of John's disciples and a certain Jew over the matter of ceremonial washing. (John 3:25)

Before and after this verse, baptism is clearly in view. Indeed, following verse 25, the disputants went to John to tell him that Jesus was also baptizing, complaining that "everyone is going to him."

In the following chapter, John 4:1-2, we are however informed that although Jesus was gaining and baptizing more disciples than John, "in fact it was not Jesus who baptized but his disciples." This is quite intriguing; why didn't Jesus baptize with water? He Himself was baptized in the river Jordan, but did not baptize anyone in water; he was circumcised, too, but did not go out of His way to circumcise those who came to Him from the Gentile communities that did not practice this rite.

There were many deeply ingrained customs and traditions that Jesus did not go out of His way to oppose; had He done so for each and every one of them, that would have distracted Him from His core mission – the salvation of mankind. The fact that He did not oppose a practice cannot be taken as a command for us to perpetuate that practice; actually, even where He did Himself undergo a rite or appear to give His approval, that cannot be taken as a command for believers to follow suit.

That is why we do not say that since Jesus was circumcised, all Christians must have the procedure performed on them. Or that because He occasionally asked those He had healed to go to the priests and perform the sacrifices commanded by Moses for their cleansing, the sick in our day are to perform animal sacrifices when God heals. The point is, whatever it is that Jesus did that was in conformity with the Law of Moses, believers have been set free from it, the defining moment having been when He died on the cross. From that time henceforth, even those who are Jewish believers are under no obligation to follow the Mosaic code.

Water baptism, then, having been part of the ceremonial washings of the Old Covenant, cannot be said to be an obligatory practice commanded of Christians.

At this juncture, we need to examine more closely the kind of baptism that John the Baptist anticipated that Jesus would initiate. In Matthew 3:11, John tells his followers: "I baptize you with water for repentance. But after me comes one who is more powerful than I, whose sandals I am not worthy to carry. He will baptize you with the Holy Spirit and with fire." John the Baptist never therefore expected the coming one to baptize with water, or first with water and then the Holy Spirit.

This point becomes even clearer when we examine John's words in Mark 1:8, "I baptize you with water, but he will baptize you with the Holy Spirit." While Luke 3:16 repeats what we have seen in Matthew and Mark, John 3:33 puts John's testimony in this interesting manner: "And I myself did not know him, but the one who sent me to baptize with water told me, 'The man on whom you see the Spirit come down and remain is the one who will baptize with the Holy Spirit.'" Thus the point is buttressed that while John the Baptist indeed baptized with water, he was under no illusion that the Messiah would similarly baptize with water, God having revealed to him clearly that the one after him would only baptize with the Holy Spirit.

This view is confirmed by the words of Christ Himself. Following his resurrection, Luke recounts in Acts 1:4-5:

On one occasion, while he was eating with them, he gave them this command: "Do not leave Jerusalem, but wait for the gift my Father promised, which you have heard me speak about. For John baptized with water, but in a few days you will be baptized with the Holy Spirit."

In full agreement with what John the Baptist had been preaching several years earlier, Jesus tells His disciples that they will be baptized with the Holy Spirit. There is absolutely no mention of water.

But one may still ask, Didn't Jesus command His followers to make disciples and baptize them when He sent them out in what has come to be known as the Great Commission? (Matthew 28:19-20). Indeed, didn't He even give them a formula, asking them to do so while reciting, "In the name of the Father and of the Son and of the Holy Spirit"? The answer to this passage can be grasped after reading the next chapter, which puts the meaning of baptism into context.

Chapter 7
Immersion or union with Christ?

It is often pointed out to new converts, quite rightly, that the word baptism is derived from the Greek word baptizo, meaning "to immerse." What is often forgotten is that words cannot be divorced from the context in which they are used. When this is done, the unfortunate result is that we end up misunderstanding the message.

Take an example of the word "eat." Everyone knows what to eat means – simply putting food in the mouth, then chewing and swallowing it. Now let us examine these words of Jesus:

> Jesus said to them, "Very truly I tell you, unless you eat the flesh of the Son of Man and drink his blood, you have no life in you. Whoever eats my flesh and drinks my blood has eternal life, and I will raise them up at the last day. For my flesh is real food and my blood is real drink. Whoever eats my flesh and drinks my blood remains in me, and I in them. Just as the living Father sent me and I live because of the Father, so the one who feeds on me will live because of me. This is the bread that came down from heaven. Your ancestors ate manna and died, but whoever feeds on this bread will live forever." (John 6:53-58)

The point Jesus was making is quite clear to us today. He simply wasn't talking about physical food! He wasn't telling his disciples to chop him up and roast his meat over a fireplace for dinner. In fact, when his disciples couldn't understand him then, he explained himself in verse 63 of the same chapter: "The Spirit gives life; the flesh counts for nothing. The words I have spoken to you – they are full of the Spirit and life."

This example demonstrates that to understand scripture, we cannot assume that the literal meaning of the words themselves gives us the intent of the Spirit. Where the context indicates a literal meaning of "eat," that's how we also are to understand it; but when the meaning is not literal, we surely cannot be at liberty to change it to a literal one. The context indicates the meaning or, if you like, the intent of the Spirit.

Back to the meaning of baptism. John's baptism was obviously one of immersion into water, in his case the river Jordan. This has unfortunately made many undiscerning Christians and bible scholars to see water whenever the word baptism is mentioned. Just as in the case of the word "eat" as examined in the example above, such an interpretation is unwarranted.

The following examples from scripture will help to illustrate this point:

(i) In Luke 12:50, Jesus says: "But I have a baptism to undergo, and what constraints I am under until it is completed." He surely wasn't thinking of returning to John the Baptist for another dip into the river Jordan! He was talking of His coming death and calling it a baptism.

(ii) Writing about the deliverance of their ancestors from the bondage of Egypt under the leadership of Moses, Paul says in 1 Corinthians 10:2: "They were all baptized into Moses in the cloud and in the sea." But, wait a minute, we have no record of

Moses conducting baptisms in the desert or in the Red Sea, so what exactly did Paul mean? All what we know is that the Israelites became followers of Moses and were instructed down the generations to follow all the laws that God passed down to them through Moses. "Baptized into Moses," then, would mean becoming a follower of Moses, or professing the beliefs and teachings of Moses – becoming of one spirit with him, so to speak.

(iii) This meaning can be ascertained from a reading of Galatians 3:26-27: "So in Christ Jesus you are all children of God through faith, for all of you who were baptized into Christ have clothed yourselves with Christ." The phrase "baptized into Christ" cannot possibly mean anything else other than to be joined with Christ, to become one with Him. It has as little to do with water as "clothed yourselves with Christ" in the same passage has to do with physical clothes.

(iv) While chastising the Corinthians for their divisions and urging them toward unity in Christ, Paul surprisingly boasts about having baptized very few people. Then he makes an even more intriguing statement about his mission, saying it had nothing to do with (water) baptism:

> Is Christ divided? Was Paul crucified for you? Were you baptized into the name of Paul? I thank God that I did not baptize any of you except Crispus and Gaius, so no one can say that you were baptized into my name. (Yes, I also baptized the household of Stephanas; beyond that, I don't remember if I baptized anyone else.) For Christ did not send me to baptize but to preach the gospel – not with wisdom and eloquence, lest the cross of Christ be emptied of its power. (1 Corinthians 1:13-17)

If water baptism is truly commanded of God, why would Paul "thank God" that he did not baptize many people instead of praying for the Lord to cause more people to come for baptism? Far from it, it is evident that Paul has come to a realization of the worthlessness of this ritual and is now thankful that He did not persist in this error for long, having baptized only a few people before coming to a realization of the truth.

Indeed, if water baptism is what Christ intended when He gave the Great Commission, and if it is of such great importance as many Christians have been made to believe, why would Paul talk so slightingly about such a practice by saying Christ did not send him to baptize? He makes clear his mission statement: to preach the gospel. He had no time for useless rituals. As he says elsewhere in Romans 1:16, "I am not ashamed of the gospel, because it is the power of God that brings salvation to everyone who believes: first to the Jew, then to the Gentile." The Holy Spirit cannot at one time in the New Testament command a ritual and then at another point trash it so badly. Truly, the only explanation is that there has been a gross misunderstanding of the intent of the Holy Spirit by picking on the letter of the words in Matthew 28:19 without searching the Spirit.

(v) The figurative way in which scripture speaks is even clearer when one examines the following passage:

What shall we say, then? Shall we go on sinning so that grace may increase? By no means! We are those who have died to sin; how can we live in it any longer? Or don't you know that all of us who were baptized into Christ Jesus were baptized into his death? We were therefore buried with him through baptism into death in order that, just as Christ was raised from the dead through the glory of the Father, we too may live a new life.

If we have been united with him in a death like his, we will certainly also be united with him in a resurrection like his. For we know that our old self was crucified with him so that the body ruled by sin might be done away with, that we should no longer be slaves to sin – because anyone who has died has been set free from sin. (Romans 6:1-7)

Now, although Paul says of believers that "our old self was crucified with him," we understand that this does not constitute a command for believers to be physically nailed to a cross upon being saved. Baptism and crucifixion are mentioned in the same breath in this passage, with absolutely no indication that one is to be treated as a spiritual reality and the other as a physical action. The point is that in the same way that believers are not expected to be crucified on a physical cross as a symbol of their crucifixion with Him, they are also not expected to be dipped under physical water as a symbol of their baptism into Christ.

It is important to note that the books of the New Testament – and indeed the whole bible – are not arranged in a chronological order according to the timeline in which they were written. In this regard, although the letter to the Romans appears first among the epistles and is placed immediately after the Acts of the Apostles and before the first letter to the Corinthians, it was actually written sometime after 1 Corinthians. Since by the time he wrote the latter Paul had come to a new realisation regarding water baptism and could mention it rather disparagingly (see point (iv) above), it follows that he could not have been referring to water baptism when he later wrote to the Romans that they had been "baptized into Christ."

(v) And just in case any believer thinks that baptism is an activity to be conducted by any human being, Paul clears the air:

"For we were all baptized by one Spirit so as to form one body – whether Jews or Greeks, slave or free – and we were all given the one Spirit to drink." (1 Corinthians 12:13)

Of course, the Spirit never poured water on anyone's forehead or pushed them down into a river to baptize them. Neither did God give His Spirit in a cup for anyone to drink. Only a mind that is so worldly as to have lost all spiritual discernment would insist, in the light of this verse, that the baptism envisioned in the New Testament has anything to do with material water.

(vi) In a rather difficult passage intended to encourage believers going through suffering and persecution, the apostle Peter tells them:

It is better, if it is God's will, to suffer for doing good than for doing evil. For Christ also suffered once for sins, the righteous for the unrighteous, to bring you to God. He was put to death in the body but made alive in the Spirit. In that state he went and made proclamation to the imprisoned spirits – to those who were disobedient long ago when God waited patiently in the days of Noah while the ark was being built. In it only a few people, eight in all, were saved through water, and this water symbolizes baptism that now saves you also – not the removal of dirt from the body but the pledge of a clear conscience toward God. It saves you by the resurrection of Jesus Christ, who has gone into heaven and is at God's right hand – with angels, authorities and powers in submission to him. (1 Peter 3:17-22)

Among other things, Peter in this passage compares the salvation of believers to that of Noah. But lest anyone should think that he is writing about water baptism, he makes clear that he is not referring to "the removal of dirt from the body." What a harsh indictment of water baptism – it can only remove dirt and is of no additional value. True baptism, to Peter, is "the pledge of a clear conscience toward God." It is this clear conscience that distinguished Noah in his day and enabled him to obey God, who saved him and his family from the flood. Believers are told that they have this same baptism "which now saves you also," meaning that God will use their union and communion with Him, which enables obedience of the type exemplified by Noah, to save them from the evils surrounding them in the same way that He had saved Noah before them.

A majority of Christians – especially evangelical groups – are agreed that water baptism cannot save, saying it is a mere outward show of an inner change. It would therefore be nonsensical for Peter to make the statement "baptism that now saves you also" if water baptism were in view. The baptism that Peter must have been thinking about was obviously union with Christ, because it is only through our union with him that we have eternal life and can claim victory over sin and death. In the words of Christ in John 15:5, "I am the vine; you are the branches. If you remain in me and I in you, you will bear much fruit; apart from me you can do nothing."

The passage above is a pointer that the same Peter who conducted water baptisms in the Acts of the Apostles later came to a new realization regarding true baptism. God is continually shedding His light upon His people and it would be wrong to think that the apostles were any different or that they had the full revelation of God right from the beginning; rather, we must trace the progression of their thoughts as they obeyed Christ and more light was revealed to them.

The Great Commission

Scripture is inspired by the Holy Spirit and cannot contradict itself. If baptism is not a physical act, we must therefore find out what Jesus meant when He appeared to give a command to the Eleven to baptize:

> "Then Jesus came to them and said, "All authority in heaven and on earth has been given to me. Therefore go and make disciples of all nations, baptizing them in the name of the Father and of the Son and of the Holy Spirit, and teaching them to obey everything I have commanded you. And surely I am with you always, to the very end of the age." (Matthew 28:18-20):

Baptism into Christ, as has been shown using the examples above, means union with the Lord. Christ, in turn, tells us that He is one with the Father, and that the Father is in Him and He in the Father (see, for example, John 14: 9-11). The Holy Spirit, on His part, is the Spirit of Christ and also the Spirit who comes from the Father (John 14:26, Romans 8:9). Now, if we are united with Christ, and Christ is one with the Father and the Holy Spirit, then it can be said that we also are one with the Father and the Spirit. In that case, when we have been baptized into Christ, we are also baptized into the Father and into the Holy Spirit, because these three are one. And so, by preaching the gospel and making disciples of all nations, the apostles will essentially be making them become one with divinity, which is the same as baptizing them into Christ, or, taking into account the reality of the Trinity, "baptizing them in (understood as into) the name of the Father and of the Son and of the Holy Spirit."

At least one major authority holds this same view regarding the meaning of "in the name" in this instance:

It is a commitment to ("in the name" is literally "into the name," implying entrance into an allegiance) the Father, the Son and the Holy Spirit, all three of whom were involved in the event of Jesus' baptism (Matthew 3:16-17). Matthew wants his readers to know that Jesus has taken his place along with the Father and the Spirit as the object of worship and commitment. Matthew's unique use of the Trinitarian formula summarizes in the more formal language of the community the essence of what Jesus had taught his disciples about God, instruction that had implied a unique relationship between Jesus and the Spirit with the Father. (Daniel G. Reid (ed), *The IVP Dictionary of the New Testament,* p99)

Jesus's command, understood this way, has nothing to do with physical water or a formula to be recited while dipping people into a pool or pouring water onto their foreheads. His words simply point to a spiritual reality of oneness with God, which He desires to be achieved through making disciples of all nations.

It is a clear principle in scripture that every matter shall be settled by the testimony of two or three witnesses (Deuteronomy 19:15, 2 Corinthians 13:1). An important teaching about a practice that is meant to be obeyed by churches across the world cannot be left to only one witness, Matthew. The Great Commission to the disciples is recorded by various witnesses in the New Testament. It is important to look at these other versions to ascertain whether any command was really given for water baptism.

(i) In Mark's record:

He said to them, "Go into all the world and preach the gospel to all creation. Whoever believes and is baptized will be saved, but whoever does not believe will be condemned. And these signs will accompany those who believe: In my name they will drive out demons; they will speak in new tongues; they will pick up snakes with their hands; and when they drink deadly poison, it will not hurt them at all; they will place their hands on sick people, and they will get well. (Mark 16:15-18)

It should be noted that Mark's record in these verses cannot be taken as authoritative due to questions of authenticity. Many bible versions actually have a disclaimer indicating that the earliest manuscripts do not contain Mark 16:9-20. Doctrinal teaching cannot be based on any part of scripture that is in doubt. Any text whose authenticity is in question can only be used for purposes of edification. In this case, therefore, Mark's record cannot be taken to be a reliable or second witness to Matthew with regard to water baptism.

(ii) The Great Commission is recorded differently by Luke:

He told them, "This is what is written: The Messiah will suffer and rise from the dead on the third day, and repentance for the forgiveness of sins will be preached in his name to all nations, beginning at Jerusalem. You are witnesses of these things. I am going to send you what my Father has promised; but stay in the city until you are clothed with power from on high." (Luke 24:46-49)

It is clear that Luke's record has nothing to support the doctrine of water baptism. If there was any such command, surely Luke would not have overlooked such an important matter.

(iii) Similarly, John has no record of water baptism being

commanded:

> Again Jesus said, "Peace be with you! As the Father has sent me, I am sending you." And with that he breathed on them and said, "Receive the Holy Spirit. If you forgive the sins of anyone, their sins are forgiven; if you do not forgive them, they are not forgiven." (John 20:21-23)

Is it possible that an important command to the church to baptize new believers in water throughout all generations henceforth would have escaped John's attention as well?

(iv) In the Acts of the Apostles, Luke gives a slightly different version of the Commission recorded earlier in his gospel account:

> He said to them: "It is not for you to know the times or dates the Father has set by his own authority. But you will receive power when the Holy Spirit comes on you; and you will be my witnesses in Jerusalem, and in all Judea and Samaria, and to the ends of the earth." (Acts 1:7-8)

Just as in his earlier record, Luke's narrative in Acts has no mention of a command to baptize believers in water. The failure to find a second witness to this command among all the witnesses to the Great Commission to support Matthew – if it is assumed that water baptism is what Matthew really meant in the first place – means that the whole doctrine stands on very shaky ground.

Chapter 8
The apostolic period

The apostles have rightly been referred to as interpreters of the gospel message. They helped to clarify and expound on what Jesus had said. After the Holy Spirit had come upon them (Acts 2), they were given power as promised by Christ to become His witnesses. The Holy Spirit was there also to teach them and to remind them of what Christ had taught (John 14:26).

It is no wonder that every church claims to be apostolic. To a greater or lesser extent, churches take on what they consider apostolic traditions. In other words, if we can show that the apostles approved of a practice, so goes this mindset, it is good and profitable for us to adhere to it too. But there is a problem with this attitude, as discussed in Chapter 3.

But why did the apostles baptize in water, given that Christ never commanded it? This can best be explained in terms of a deficient understanding based on their entrapment to deeply ingrained Judaic practices. As is common with all human beings, there are things the apostles simply assumed and did without any command or sanction from Christ. It would have been asking too much of them to completely and suddenly cut off every link they had with Judaism. But we who have the advantage of looking back in time should not be encumbered by practices of the apostles based on their social milieu that have nothing to do with the gospel.

As discussed earlier in Chapter 3, baptism as practised at the time of Jesus and the apostles was a continuation of the ceremonial washings of Judaism as decreed by Moses. Thus this practice – as well as others with similar roots that we may encounter in the pages of the New Testament – should be safely ignored by the discerning Christian without bringing about any pangs of conscience.

Water baptisms in the Acts of the Apostles

Luke recounts in the opening lines of the book of Acts the words of Jesus Christ to his disciples: "For John baptized with water, but in a few days you will be baptized with the Holy Spirit" (Acts 1:5). These words are as clear as it can get: No water baptism is envisioned.

However, because of the apostles' captivity to their traditions, Peter and the rest of the apostles – obviously without thinking much about these words of Christ – preach and act in the following chapter in a manner that mixes up the two distinct baptisms. They fail to acknowledge that one form of baptism was passing away and is not commanded for the future:

> Repent and be baptized, everyone of you, in the name of Jesus Christ for the forgiveness of your sins. And you will receive the gift of the Holy Spirit… Those who accepted his message were baptized, and about three thousand were added to their number that day." (Acts 2:38-41)

The Lord certainly baptized the three thousand people who believed in Him on the day of Pentecost – He united them to

Himself through His Spirit. But the other baptism that was done in water had nothing to do with God – it was simply borne of human tradition.

In Acts 8:26ff, we encounter Philip evangelizing to the Ethiopian eunuch. At the end of it all, the eunuch joyfully believes in Jesus, but then asks:

> "Look, here is water, what can stand in the way of my being baptized? And he gave orders to stop the chariot. Then both Philip and the eunuch went down into the water and Philip baptized him." (Acts 8:37-38)

It was the eunuch himself who campaigned to be baptized in water! The Lord did not command that the new believer be so baptized. Perhaps, had Philip understood the nature of the true spiritual baptism, he would have advised the eunuch that water baptism was unnecessary. Or he may have chosen not to stand in the new convert's way, focusing on what was important and letting the eunuch please himself on such a mundane matter. Either way, although Philip gave in to the request for water baptism on this occasion, there is no command from God about this being a necessary rite for believers.

Fast forward to the house of Cornelius in Acts 10. The Lord has miraculously revealed himself to Cornelius and Peter; finally, Peter preaches to the household of Cornelius. And then something extraordinary happens:

> While Peter was still speaking these words, the Holy Spirit came on all who heard the message. The circumcised believers who had come with Peter were astonished that the gift of the Holy Spirit had been poured out even on Gentiles. For they heard them speaking in tongues and praising God.

Then Peter said, "Surely no one can stand in the way of their being baptized with water. They have received the Holy Spirit just as we have." So he ordered that they be baptized in the name of Jesus Christ. Then they asked Peter to stay with them for a few days. (Acts 10:44-48)

In this instance, the Lord did His bit – the Holy Spirit's presence was evident as the Lord consummated His union with these believers, so to speak. He became one with them through the baptism of the Holy Spirit. But being a man given to the flesh, Peter wanted more: a ritual. The Lord did not command that Cornelius and his household be put through a charade of water baptism; it is Peter who ordered that this be done. In his carnality, he imagined that the baptism of the Holy Spirit was incomplete without man adding something to it, hence the rite of water baptism.

With the seed of water baptism having been planted, it grew. The baptisms of Paul, Lydia and others narrated in the Acts of the Apostles simply followed the assumptions and patterns erroneously planted by the apostles. Man's effort was seen as necessary to make the new birth complete. This is the lie that has grown throughout Christendom to this day in the form of water baptism.

It is this mix-up in understanding that explains the following events in Ephesus:

While Apollos was at Corinth, Paul took the road through the interior and arrived at Ephesus. There he found some disciples and asked them, "Did you receive the Holy Spirit when you believed?
They answered, "No, we have not even heard that there is a Holy Spirit.
So Paul asked, "Then what baptism did you receive?"

"John's baptism," they replied.

Paul said, "John's baptism was a baptism of repentance. He told the people to believe in the one coming after him, that is, in Jesus." On hearing this, they were baptized into the name of the Lord Jesus. When Paul placed his hands on them, the Holy Spirit came on them, and they spoke in tongues and prophesied. There were about twelve men in all. (Acts 19:1-7)

If these disciples had not even heard that there is a Holy Spirit, they were evidently not disciples of Jesus Christ. They themselves readily say that they had received John's baptism. Paul correctly interprets for them what John's baptism signified – it was simply a baptism of repentance and a precursor to the true baptism given by Jesus Christ: John the Baptist did not preach about himself, but rather the one coming after him.

Everything is clear up to this point. John's disciples receive the witness of the Holy Spirit and accept Paul's message, for no one can accept the message of Christ without the Father drawing him to do so. But then Paul falls into the common error of requiring them to perform a human ritual, a repetition of the very baptism of John that he has so ably renounced.

Finally, Paul places his hands on them. As a result, Luke says that, "They spoke in tongues and prophesied." The water baptism that Paul and the apostles practised is what has come to be known as "believers' baptism." To believe, one must be convicted by the Holy Spirit. These believers already had the Holy Spirit dwelling within them. What happened when Paul placed his hands on them is that they received spiritual gifts that enabled them to begin speaking in tongues and prophesying. The Holy Spirit manifested Himself in specific outward ways in their lives; however, as far as union with Christ (or baptism in Christ) is concerned, they had received this immediately they believed.

Did water baptism by the apostles impart grace?

Among those who practice water baptism, there are some who believe that the rite confers a special grace for living the Christian life. This has been shown to be a lie right from the early apostolic period.

The story of Simon the Sorcerer (as recounted in Acts 8:9-24) is instructive. This man, who was a well-known sorcerer, "believed and was baptized." But because his heart was still not right with God, when He saw that the Spirit's manifestation was evident when Peter and John laid their hands on some believers, he offered them money as a bribe so that he could acquire the same power. His old nature of manipulative witchcraft had not been overcome; he had simply moved with it into his new-found faith.

This example right from scripture is ample evidence that there is no grace to be found in water baptism. Water baptism cannot bring about any grace or empowerment for Christian living. Where change has occurred and the fruit of a believer's faith is evident to all around him, such a change cannot be ascribed to water baptism; rather, it is due to the inner working of God's Spirit in the person's life.

Chapter 9
A second baptism of the Holy Spirit?

Pentecostal and charismatic groups generally believe in a second major event following conversion in which the Holy Spirit comes down upon believers. They call this the baptism of (or in or by) the Holy Spirit. This second infilling is supposed to be accompanied by speaking in tongues.

The evidence for this doctrine is obtained from the Book of Acts. It is pointed out that whenever the Holy Spirit came down upon believers, the evidence was tongues. Thus, adherents to this teaching would urge every Christian to desire this second experience. Spirit-filled believers are those who speak in tongues, it is claimed.

This position betrays a confusion of terms: The gift promised to the disciples and subsequently all believers is that of the Holy Spirit, not tongues.

> On one occasion, while he was eating with them, he gave them this command: "Do not leave Jerusalem, but wait for the gift my Father promised, which you have heard me speak about. For John baptized with water, but in a few days you will be baptized with the Holy Spirit." (Acts 1:4-5)

Peter replied, "Repent and be baptized, every one of you, in the name of Jesus Christ for the forgiveness of your sins. And you will receive the gift of the Holy Spirit." (Acts 2:38)

It is true that when the Holy Spirit came down on the disciples in Acts 2:4, they began to speak in other tongues as the Holy Spirit enabled them. But this is a bad foundation on which to build a theology of a baptism of the Holy Spirit accompanied by tongues. It should be carefully noted that this is the only instance in the New Testament where the tongues spoken constituted other intelligible languages understood by actual linguistic groups. Later tongues, such as those spoken in Corinth, were not in the same league, as Paul's words clearly show:

Now, brothers and sisters, if I come to you and speak in tongues, what good will I be to you, unless I bring some revelation or knowledge or prophecy or word of instruction?... Unless you speak intelligible words with your tongue, how will anyone know what you are saying? You will just be speaking into the air... Since you are eager for gifts of the Spirit, try to excel in those that build up the church. (1 Corinthians 14:6-12)

It is also important to note that the prophecy of Joel that Peter refers to in Acts 2:17-21 speaks of many other manifestations of the same Spirit when He is given out: prophecy, visions, dreams, and wonders in heaven and on earth. At the conclusion of Peter's message, we are told that three thousand people came to Christ (Acts 2:41), but we are not told whether they too spoke in tongues.

The Holy Spirit was behind the evangelization of the Ethiopian eunuch, but we are not told if he spoke in tongues or even prophesied. His heart of a seeker and passion are however evident, and we are told that "he went on his way rejoicing." (Acts 8:39) There are numerous other recorded events where the apostles evangelized but tongues are not mentioned.

At Cornelius's household, Luke records that the Jewish believers were astonished to hear Peter's audience "speaking in tongues and praising God." There is no insinuation that they all spoke in tongues. The same applies to the twelve disciples of John whom Paul encountered in Acts 19:1-7; we cannot say for sure that each of them must have spoken in tongues as well as prophesied.

From the aforegoing, it can be said that speaking in tongues is not a necessary gift when the Spirit comes down upon someone. In order to arrive at the truth regarding this matter, it is important to look at the whole counsel of scripture rather than selectively at those passages that appear to advance a preferred line of thought. Regarding gifting, Paul asks the Corinthians a series of rhetorical questions:

> Are all apostles? Are all prophets? Are all teachers? Do all work miracles? Do all have gifts of healing? Do all speak in tongues? Do all interpret? (1 Corinthians 12:28-29)

The answer to this series of questions is undoubtedly "No." It cannot be "No" to all the other questions except the one touching on tongues.

Later in the same epistle, it becomes clear that there were believers who spoke in tongues in Corinth but did not prophesy and vice versa, meaning tongues is not an essential gift for every believer. It is also clearly less valued than prophecy:

Follow the way of love and eagerly desire spiritual gifts, especially the gift of prophecy. For those who speak in a tongue do not speak to other people but to God. Indeed, no one understands them; they utter mysteries by the Spirit. But those who prophesy speak to people for their strengthening, encouragement and comfort. Those who speak in a tongue edify themselves, but those who prophesy edify the church. I would like everyone of you to speak in tongues, but I would rather have you prophesy. Those who prophesy are greater than those who speak in tongues, unless they interpret, so that the church may be edified. (1 Corinthians 14:1-5)

This is not to say that tongues is not a valid gift of the Holy Spirit, or that the gift has ceased as some denominations teach. Like everything that God gives, tongues is a wonderful gift, no doubt about that. But we must also value every gift of the Holy Spirit and we should neither elevate tongues beyond its rightful position nor consider inconsequential the differing gifts of others: "There are different kinds of gifts, but the same Spirit distributes them (1 Corinthians 12:4)."

It is unfortunate that one manifestation of the Holy Spirit has been confused with the actual reception of the Spirit. It should be clear to all believers that the Holy Spirit is received at the moment of salvation, when God is pleased to call us to Himself and to work out our faith to respond to Him. At that time, we are instantly united with our Lord and receive the seal of His Spirit. That's true baptism.

At the moment of our union with Him or even thereafter, God may be pleased to grant us gifts according to His grace and purposes in our lives. These gifts may or may not include tongues (or glossolalia). The gift of tongues, therefore, is distinctly different from the baptism of the Holy Spirit, or baptism into Christ, which occurs at the moment of salvation. The granting of the gift of tongues, or of any other gift for that matter, does not constitute the baptism of the Holy Spirit.

Max Turner elaborates on the weakness of the Pentecostal worldview propagating a two-stage reception of the Holy Spirit:

> Modern contributions to the debate appear increasingly to support the view that we cannot split the giving of the Spirit into two distinct successive stages... Those who have had a crisis 'Spirit-baptism' of some kind, beyond conversion, may have further, sometimes more dramatic, experiences of empowering, but this does not provide the basis for Pentecostal theologies of third, fourth and fifth-stage 'receptions' of the Spirit... We do not have the empirical grounds for a rigidly two-stage paradigm of Spirit-reception. 'Pentecostal' experiences are then better explained as single events within a potentially multiple-occasion series of renewal or empowering experiences of the one gift of the Spirit granted in conversion-initiations... An experience of receiving tongues, or some other charism, accompanied by, for example, a heightened sense of the presence of God, does not mark entry into some different realm of the Spirit, but is simply part and parcel of the all-encompassing work of renewal and re-creation which the believer experiences, in a variety of fruit and charisms, from the beginning of Christian life. What Pentecostals experienced as a second-stage 'Spirit-baptism' should thus be understood as just one of potentially many 'growth experiences' in the charismatic Spirit given in conversion-initiation rather than the normative mode of entry to some decisively new realm

of the Spirit. (Max Turner, *The Holy Spirit and Spiritual Gifts Then and Now*, Paternoster Press, 1999, p158-163)

By confusing a specific manifestation of the Holy Spirit with the baptism of the Holy Spirit, Pentecostals have lost sight of the true baptism that occurs at salvation. In its place, they have created two baptisms: one of water and another that accurately points to the true baptism in its name but describes an altogether different reality.

In doing so, Pentecostal leaders have misled multitudes into focusing on physical phenomena for the presence and blessing of God rather than the fruit of the Holy Spirit. This easily leads believers down the path of mind control and exploitation, where they think tongues and miracles are what matter. Such Christians become easy prey for demons. I have dealt with conmen who go about their trade as they speak in tongues and prophesy; I have also seen the warmth and love of Christians who exhibited none of these two gifts but whose lives portray Christ's presence and glory.

A theology that focuses on outward manifestation is a logical step from the first error of thinking God is pleased with an external washing ceremony in the name of baptism. So, one error on the matter of water baptism breeds another in the form of a misguided doctrine of the baptism of the Holy Spirit.

A theology of two baptisms, moreover, fails to reconcile itself with the truth outlined earlier in Chapter 2 that there can indeed be only one baptism – as so categorically pronounced by Paul in Ephesians 4:4-6. When we find ourselves with two or more baptisms to contend with, that should be reason enough for any Christian to pause and reflect. As it has been demonstrated, both concepts of baptism are false.

An insistence on tongues can serve to create a feeling of inferiority on those who have equally received the Spirit but have a different gifting. Conversely, it creates a superiority complex on the part of those with the gift of tongues.

The baptism of the Holy Spirit at the moment of salvation empowers God's people for the Christian life and witness. The dilution of this truth can only weaken Christians in their individual walk and collective witness, as Spirit-filled believers fail to recognize the power within them and wait instead for an ecstatic experience of glossolalia. The spectacle of such Christians must be extremely pleasing to Satan.

The formulation of a doctrine of a multi-stage Christianity can only be harmful to the body of Christ. One must first say a sinner's prayer, followed by water baptism, followed by a "baptism of the Holy Spirit" to be evidenced by speaking in tongues. Beyond faith in Jesus Christ, it appears, one has to put in a lot of other effort to be at peace with God! That obviously cannot be true.

The doctrine of a second baptism of the Holy Spirit practised by most Pentecostal and charismatic groups cannot stand the scrutiny of scripture. It is not a valid baptism, but simply signifies the reception of spiritual gifts by Christians who have already been baptized by the Holy Spirit from the moment of conversion.

Chapter 10
The effect of water baptism on the church

A s with all traditions that man has become accustomed
to and is unwilling to let go, the question arises: What
harm is there in water baptism? Granted, the practice is
Judaic in origin and is not commanded by the Lord, but why not
just let it be? After all, we are all happy with the situation as it is,
so why rock the boat?

A lot of harm results from this carefree attitude in the body
of Christ, where anything goes and anyone who so wishes goes
ahead to misuse their liberty without anybody else giving a loving word of correction. We must always seek to clearly discern
what the Lord wants.

And so, what the Lord desires for His church should be our
first ground for rejecting water baptism. Jesus said that, "Every
plant that my heavenly Father has not planted will be pulled up
by the roots" (Matthew 15:13). If we are sure that the Father did
not plant a clergy-laity divide, it is our responsibility to do all
we can to uproot it from our midst; He did not plant a denomi-

national system, so we uproot that too; neither did He did plant liturgies and orders of worship, so that goes out as well. By a proper exegesis, He did not plant water baptism either, and that is reason enough for that to go out of the window, too.

The book of Revelation puts the same point differently but with finality about the dire consequences of adding or subtracting to what God has ordained:

I warn everyone who hears the words of the prophecy of this scroll: If any one of you adds anything to them, God will add to you the plagues described in this scroll. And if any one of you takes words away from this scroll of prophecy, God will take away from you your share in the tree of life and in the Holy City, which are described in this scroll. (Revelation 22:18-19)

This is a warning that should make us shudder any time we are tempted to take lightly any addition we have made to our faith. It should make us eager to reflect on all that we do, including all those things that we take for granted, and bring them to the scrutiny of Scripture. As God sheds light on the church, we cannot but uproot every plant that the heavenly Father has not planted. That includes water baptism.

Water baptism destroys the distinction between Jesus followers and the disciples of worldly systems of religion. Jesus brought into the world a radically different way of perceiving and doing things for His followers. He did not bring to us yet another religious system to compete with those already in the world and those other that might emerge. No, what He initiated was so radical that it could be said that "friendship with the world means enmity against God." (James 4:4)

Anyone who reads the gospels with just a little discernment will see that our Master constantly opposed the religious leaders and systems of His day. In turn, the Pharisees and teachers of the law were constantly on his trail, asking all kinds of questions to see if they could trap him or, better still, kill him. There was no love lost between Jesus and religious systems. How can we, who claim to follow Jesus, now bind ourselves to religious thinking and systems so completely without batting an eyelid?

Jesus spoke slightingly about those who perform religious duties in order to attract the approval of men:

> Everything they do is done for people to see: They make their phylacteries wide and the tassels on their garments long; they love the place of honour at banquets and the most important seats in the synagogues; they love to be greeted with respect in the marketplaces and to have people call them 'Rabbi.' (Matthew 23:5-7)

In the same chapter of Matthew, Jesus goes on to call the religious leaders of his day names: hypocrites, white-washed tombs, snakes and so forth. It is therefore quite certain that neither Jesus nor the apostles established any system of religion. And even though some religious rituals may have persisted at the time of the apostles, we are not justified to continue following their lead any more than we may ask slaves to obey their masters.

By turning faith in Jesus Christ into just another religious system with a hierarchy, sacred temples, holy days, holy sites, rituals and ceremonies, we diminish the glory of Christ and put him on the same pedestal as any other founder of religion. Such a religion, even though it may be called Christianity, cannot be said to draw its power or example from Christ. On the contrary, the religion of Christianity as described here is simply part and parcel of the world system.

How can this be so? Christianity has tried to ape the world system to the fullest extent. Because other religions have magnificent temples and mosques, Christianity tries to outdo them and conveniently ignores the teaching that the body of believers constitutes the true temple of the Holy Spirit.

Since the world system teaches that bigger is better, the religious system of Christianity also competes on the same terms, with more followers and increased temporal power being taken as a sign of God's approval. But anyone who studies the bible closely will find that the way of the cross is a way of suffering and ignominy. No wonder the prophets, apostles and others who have dared to follow God have met the wrath of the world system and have paid with their very lives. Yet, counterfeit Christianity pretends that worldly standards can be a measure of spiritual victory. This makes it possible for those who are not ready to pay the cost of discipleship to deceive themselves that they are indeed followers of Christ.

And in the same manner that the world fights its wars of conquest, so does this behemoth of counterfeit Christianity fight – leading to Inquisitions, crusades, burnings at the stake, forced baptisms and massacres. The weirdest hermeneutics in interpreting the Old Testament wars of the Israelites are used to justify such atrocities, forgetting the clear message of the New Testament that we are to love even our enemies and that we do not fight using the weapons of this world:

> For our struggle is not against flesh and blood, but against the rulers, against the authorities, against the powers of this dark world and against the spiritual forces of evil in the heavenly realms. (Ephesians 6:12).

Paul thereafter describes the armor of God in human terms for the sake of analogy, but it amounts to a gross misinterpretation of that great apostle's message to imagine that he sanctions fighting by the use of physical swords and armor.

Physical battles are of the world; the Christian fights spiritual battles. Everything the Christian does with regard to his faith, from the moment of his salvation to his entry into heaven, is done in the spiritual realm. To cultivate the thinking that there is a physical dimension mediated by man through the use of material elements is to go into error. But right from baptism and extending to prayers for the dead, this deception that man has spiritual power over God's work runs deep. It is borne of an inability to trust God fully and hence seeks to put man in control of events. That manipulative spirit of control is no better than witchcraft.

As is known from the record of church history, the cost of this erroneous mindset has been enormous. This is not only in terms of wars and atrocities, but more fundamentally the propagation of numerous false doctrines, some of which are discussed in the next few chapters but whose genesis is a focus on the material at the expense of the spiritual.

It is not to be doubted that there are Christians who have undergone water baptism but have also been baptized into Christ, which is the baptism that matters. To such believers, one baptism was worthless, the other of lasting and eternal value. But lest we forget, the work of the counterfeit is always to devalue the authentic. It becomes difficult for the Christian to maintain his focus and integrity of faith when a deliberate seed of confusion is sown: Where church and temple are no longer a spiritual reality of the body of Christ but a physical cathedral; the cross ceases to signify death to sin and becomes a mere adornment; the priesthood is no longer a reference to all Christians collectively but an upper caste of Christians; and baptism is not union with Christ but a dipping into water.

When such spiritual realities are brought into the physical realm, with the passage of time we lose sight of the meaning of the original realities. The physical aspect that brings in human traditions and rituals to the spiritual reality is of hardly any lasting value. However, it is a way of aiding the enemy, whether deliberately or inadvertently, by sowing confusion among the brethren.

Many church planters have often expressed the opinion that water baptism is a way of evangelizing the lost. That may be so, but it would be evangelizing using a bad foundation. It would be akin to committing murder with the aim of getting jailed and reaching the convicts in prison for Jesus. Though this may seem a far-fetched example, yet the point is clear that good cannot have evil as its foundation. Otherwise, every church tradition down the ages can be justified by looking at some good. Why, cathedrals built using funds extorted from the poor have been helpful in providing shelter to people fleeing war; Christian denominations in many countries, founded as they are upon an unscriptural division of the church, do run innumerable charitable institutions; and the clergy, who form an unbiblical upper caste of Christians, have brought many people to Christ around the world. But such good – even the presence of well-meaning Christians ignorantly belonging to religious systems – should never blind us to the foundational rot nor tempt us to overlook it. It should be possible, then, to preach the gospel without recourse to practices that are inimical to the very gospel that we are preaching.

When people come to faith in Jesus Christ and one of the very first things we do is to introduce them to a ritual – thus reducing spiritual realities to physical phenomena – we set a bad precedent for their spiritual growth. That seed then germinates and grows, creating carnal Christians who always think of God in physical terms. If to get to Christ one needs water, then surely one can also use money to obtain His favour; if another human being is necessary to bring one into the church using the rite of water baptism, then surely it is important to have someone who listens to God on our behalf and tells us on weekly basis what the Almighty God is saying through a Sunday sermon; if water is of such importance in the kingdom of God, certainly oil – particularly some expensive olive oil – must be even more important.

Rather than moving people closer to God, then, the implantation of a carnal attitude only makes the new believer veer off into a different course. It moves believers into the realm of superstition; is it any wonder that so many Christians are ready to part with a fortune to con preachers whose tools of trade are oil, water and even simple soil?

This is not to say that God in His sovereign power cannot use such elements to achieve His purposes. However, in the New Testament, we see signs and wonders – say the use of Paul's handkerchiefs and Peter's shadow – being used to bring unbelievers to Christ. Believers, who are already children of God, are not the target of such signs and wonders. When Christians and unbelievers alike are called upon to behold miracles and the focus is not Christ but the glory of some televangelist, then the motives for such miracles and the power behind them becomes suspect. But Christians who have been encouraged to take on a worldly perspective from the first day of their new birth can hardly discern anything amiss.

No doubt, by creating the expectation that somebody else must do something to them for their Christian walk to be complete, the priesthood of the new believer is perverted. Instead of being encouraged to take their stand as God's children in a direct relationship with the Father, believers come to view intermediaries as important. If one needs another person to baptize them into union with God, it may be that it is also necessary, after all, to need such a person for transmitting their prayers; or to receive some token bread and wine or juice from that person for their continued healthy communion with God; or to seek the services of one who is older in the faith to lay hands on them for some spiritual purpose to be achieved. Such an attitude of dependency upon others removes the believer's focus from Jesus and places it on people, especially those who are perceived to be spiritually superior. It is a mind that is antithetical to New Testament teaching and has taken the evil genius of the powers of hell to bring about.

The Christian belief in salvation by grace through faith in Jesus Christ also becomes a casualty. If to be fully Christian one needs another human being to baptize them in water, then surely our own actions and righteousness are important before God, the Christian will reason. In actual fact, while preaching salvation through grace alone, many denominations will burden the new believer with a whole set of conditions: water baptism, which sometimes has to be repeated in accordance with the rules of the new sect if one is moving from another denomination; tithes, first fruits and all sorts of offerings; attendance of Sunday services; uniforms, in some denominations; and membership of cell groups, among others.

The impact of these conditions is to erode the new believer's newfound freedom in Jesus Christ, quickly turning him into a slave of men. Salvation becomes unattractive to those outside and a difficult walk for those inside. The words of Paul to the Galatians ring true:

> I would like to learn just one thing from you: Did you receive the Spirit by observing the law, or by believing what you heard? Are you so foolish? After beginning with the Spirit, are you now trying to finish by human effort? (Galatians 3:2-3).

Although Paul's concern was with the Galatians' drift back to the Law of Moses, his words are true of all man-made laws.

And while water baptism may appear innocent in all this, it provides the initial seed in departing from salvation by grace through faith in Jesus Christ alone. We need, like in the days of Paul, to reaffirm that we receive the Spirit by believing what is heard (the gospel), not by observing the law (baptism and all other conditions imposed by men).

Of even greater importance is that the attitude of giving premium to our own actions is despicable before God. When we start thinking that we can do anything either on our own or in collaboration with others in order to merit His grace and favour, we reduce salvation to something we can work for, not a gift. Water baptism is normally the first of many actions that inculcate this erroneous frame of mind. The believer should simply know that He has been saved and nothing more is necessary to make him complete.

Sadly, some sects have made it part of their doctrine that without baptism there can be no salvation. According to the Catechism of the Catholic Church, "The Lord himself affirms that Baptism is necessary for salvation." Giving this practice a high place in the Christian life, it goes on to say: "Holy Baptism is the basis of the whole Christian life, the gateway to life in the Spirit... Through Baptism we are freed from sin and reborn as sons of God; we become members of Christ, are incorporated into the Church and made sharers in her mission."

Regarding infant baptism, the catechism pronounces: "Children also have need of the new birth in Baptism to be freed from the power of darkness and brought into the realm of the freedom of the children of God, to which all men are called." Thus, a mere human ritual is accorded divine power that attempts to usurp God's authority to forgive sins. A ritual takes the place of saving grace, making entry into heaven the prerogative of humans. What a grand deception.

Different Christian denominations have created various variants of baptism. Many place much less emphasis than Catholics on the role of baptism in matters of faith, but still hold it as an important initiatory rite in what they perceive as obedience to the Great Commission. Most of these groups take water baptism to be an outward sign of the inner change that has taken place. Some accept new members from other denominations without the need to repeat water baptism, while others insist on a new rite, especially if it is done in a significantly different way in the denomination that the believer is moving from. There is therefore no discernible unity among believers on issues to do with baptism. The Salvation Army and Quakers do not practice baptism; this does not mean an absence of other legalisms, though.

Some commentators have expressed the opinion that water baptism has provided a means of a new believer's renunciation of their previous life and identification with the rest of the body of Christ right from the early days of the church:

> "In this way, new believers identified with others and committed themselves to that local house church in worship and service, whether it was in Jerusalem, Corinth, Colossae, Rome or elsewhere. Baptism was the rite of entry into the church. For the early believers this was a serious and monumental decision, because it separated them from unbelievers and identified them with the Christian community." (Arthur G. Patzia, *The Emergence of the Church*, p241.)

In an era and geographical region where baptism provided the rite for "initiating people into certain religious societies or organizations (Patzia, p231)," this reasoning probably made some sense. As with most traditions, it came to be senselessly extended to all cultures and peoples throughout the world, most of whom had no such rite, or had different initiatory rites that would have made more sense in the local set-up so long as these local practices were not repugnant to Christian beliefs. So much for legalistic thinking.

This sort of reasoning also begs the question: How should Christians seek to be recognized in society? It is simplistic to suggest that a ritual method of seeking recognition and identification is effective for a valid Christian witness. The secret to identifying His followers was provided by the Lord Jesus Christ Himself:

> A new command I give you: Love one another. As I have loved you, so you must love one another. By this everyone will know that you are my disciples, if you love one another. (John 13:34-35).

Love creates a bond of unity among believers that is immediately evident to the whole world and cannot be hidden. It is the distinguishing mark of the genuine Christian and the true church. Where this is evident, the Lord guarantees that there will be "much fruit, showing yourselves to be my disciples (John 15:8)"

Given our Lord's clear words about how the world will come to know His followers, we must then ask ourselves: Has it become so difficult for us to fulfill His instructions that we are seeking a clever way out of the divine command by creating our own traditions? Thus Pharisaic Christians nullify the command of God for the sake of their own traditions. They show little concern for the poor and oppressed, yet count themselves as "Christians" just because someone has dunked them in water. This way, they can assuage their consciences by blurring the lines between false brethren and true Christians. The world sees through such hypocrisy and scoffs at it. Unfortunately, many unbelievers end up thinking that all Christians are like that. Far from enhancing the Christian witness, it is destroyed.

Not only this, but traditions have a way of distorting the way we view the scriptures, even on matters that should be quite obvious. Consider the following statement by an acknowledged authority that is widely used by bible scholars and seminarians:

The NT affords neither precept nor precedent for the administration of baptism except by an ordained minister. From an early period, however, laymen did give baptism where ministers were not available. (Walter A. Elwell (ed), *Evangelical Dictionary of Theology,* second edition, p134)

One lie leads to another, every distortion serves as a building block for the next. To consider ordination an apostolic practice is to stretch the imagination, for the New Testament has no such ritual. Neither is there any evidence of a divide between the clergy and laity; this is wholly unbiblical. Again, it is nowhere mentioned or insinuated that water baptism as practiced in the New Testament was the preserve of a certain category of Christians. The writer has simply read back his denominational biases into the bible. This shows how significantly an apparently innocent ritual has contributed to distortion of the Word of God.

Once this evil seed of selective interpretation to suit man's desires has been planted, the cancer quickly spreads to all other areas of the faith. To support a hierarchical structure within the religious system, scripture will be distorted so as to make the claim that the three persons of the Godhead are themselves in a hierarchical relationship, while ignoring all evidence to the contrary. To justify the lower position accorded women in the denominational set-up, verses about submission and silence will be played up, while refusing to take the same hard stance with regard to slavery due to today's societal ethical consciousness;

verses that mention a lack of gender distinction in the church are quickly buried under. The word of God is reduced to something to be manipulated by man, thereby stifling its power.

It is this tendency that has led to the multiplicity of false doctrines seen in the church today. Unlike the encouragement of the scriptures that is always focused on Christ, the sermons, books and songs of today's false churches are preoccupied with seeking material riches. It is not to say that Christ does not care about material deprivation, it is just that this is never the main focus of scripture. So obvious is the materialistic mindset that even outsiders who know little about Christianity can see through some of the deception. A few of these false teachings that are the result of this warped mindset are covered in the next three chapters.

In terms of principles of interpretation, the practice of water baptism contributes to the erroneous impression among Christians that all what the apostles or other disciples said or did in the New Testament record is normative for the church. This has resulted in much disagreement. Such a hermeneutic, when applied consistently, would demand that the Christian must abstain from certain foodstuffs as commanded by the apostles to the Gentile churches in Acts 15:20 and 29; that we must observe 3pm as an hour of prayer as the apostles did in Acts 3:1; that we must share unleavened bread and wine in our gatherings just as the apostolic churches did; that Christian women must cover their heads; and that those who are consigned to slave-like conditions in our capitalist systems must remain content with their situation. The freedom that Christ purchased for all believers therefore goes up in flames at the altar of the letter without the Spirit.

This slave mentality must be fought from the very beginning of the Christian life by exposing every counterfeit baptism and insisting only on the invisible baptism of the Spirit. We can then focus the Christian on following the same course of the Spirit in every matter: That one should be ready to give up food or other rights for the sake of other people's sensitivities; that every time is an hour of prayer and we simply follow the Lord's leading; that we will joyfully share with others whatever food and drink God provides within our own cultural settings; that Christian women as well as men ought to maintain modesty and decency in dress and manners so as not to offend others, as defined by the societies in which we live; and that we must actively do all that is in our power to help the poor and to fight social injustices.

Baptism creates a perception of classes of Christians, a two-stage Christianity. Upon giving my life to Christ, I remember that I had to endure months of anxiety before I finally underwent water baptism. I kept wondering when I would be baptized and never stopped making enquiries. I somehow felt that I was not fully obedient without undergoing the ritual. Before going for the ritual, I also had to go through some baptismal classes for a couple of weeks. In retrospect, of course, I realize that this anxiety was totally uncalled for, yet it caused me such unnecessary heartache at that time. The wait and anguish must be much worse for those who have to memorize the prayers and dogmas contained in catechisms before they can be considered qualified for the ritual. When the so-called baptism of the Holy Spirit as evidenced by tongues is added into the mix, this unwarranted caste system in Christianity gets as bad as it can be.

It is quite common to hear Christians of all persuasions measure the success of evangelistic efforts by the numbers of people baptized. This is surprising, since it should be quite obvious that baptismal numbers do not necessarily translate into transformed lives. With the benefit of two millennia of Christianity, we ought to know that multitudes of "Christians" have not faired much better than Simon the sorcerer: The burnings on the stake, the persecutions of the Waldenses and Albigenses, papal intrigues and power plays, the crusades, the slave trade, the world wars... the list of disasters perpetrated by water-baptized "Christians" is endless.

While there is urgency to spread the gospel to all people groups throughout the world, the preoccupation with numbers of those baptized is often misleading and is best resisted, for "The Lord knows those who are His (2 Timothy 2:19)." If indeed one desires data on those who have heard and accepted the message of Christ, this can easily be obtained anyway without the rite of baptism. It is then possible to follow up on various churches to find out about their health, growth and Christian witness. The point here is that undue emphasis on the numbers of baptismal candidates brings about a distorted view of the strength of a church and evangelistic success.

The fruit of water baptism has been bitter. The theological arguments that have resulted from this practice have divided Christians for absolutely no reason. Worse still, they have led not only to forced baptisms but also such horrors as the burning of heretics on the stake, raising doubt whether many of those who advocate for this and other traditions really know Christ in the first place.

It is saddening to consider the effort, time and resources that have been expended over the centuries for the sake of this worthless ritual. Construction of baptismal pools, printing of cards, the many books that have been published advocating one form or the other of water baptism as more biblically valid... the list of wastages is endless. What if all these resources had been used for more worthwhile purposes – would the world not be a better place? I venture to suggest that such efforts would have had a lot more impact for the gospel had they been focused on helping the poor or supporting missionary activity to take the gospel to the ends of the earth.

For genuine Christians who desire a loving relationship with others, the question should not be whether to practice infant or believers baptism, whether to do so using the name of Jesus or that of the Trinity, or whether to conduct the rite by immersion or sprinkling. The issue is: Why baptize at all? Why not be satisfied with the baptism conducted by the Holy Spirit Himself, believing it to be sufficient for every believer? Once it is grasped that water baptism is neither commanded nor of any value to the Christian life, all other positions and shades of opinion regarding the intricacies of the practice can be seen for what they are: worthless arguments and mere sideshows.

Chapter 11
False teachings: Tithing

I n this and the next two chapters, I will examine a few of the common but erroneous teachings of our time. Naturally, a thorough treatment of the matter of false doctrines, whether throughout the centuries or even just in our day, would require several volumes. Many good books are available that deal with some of the most common errors. However, a practice such as tithing is so widespread that it is proper to include it in this book as well. Some of the other false practices examined in the next few chapters, such as the misuse of the blood of Jesus, have not been fully explored in many works.

The abolition of the Law of Moses, of which tithing is a part, was discussed in Chapter 3. This chapter builds on the material there by looking specifically at tithing in the Old Testament and what the New Testament has to say about giving.

Probably no other teaching has been as divisive of the church and done more harm to it in modern times than the false doctrine of tithing. A majority of Christians have actually grown up in their faith thinking that tithing is a normal part of Christian life and commanded in the Bible. The resulting abuse in the Body of Christ has been phenomenal. But does a proper understanding of the verses that address the issue of tithing command this practice for the New Covenant believer?

Believers have been called robbers; they have been denied privileges and pastoral services for not being faithful tithers; and church membership is tied to tithing in many denominations. Under such pressure, many are the Christians who have despaired in their spiritual walk, wondering whether God really cares or is just after their money. They have ended up condemning themselves and destroying, to varying degrees, their walk with the Lord.

The tithe in its original context

If we start reading the famous verses on robbing God in Malachi from just a couple of verses earlier, we get to know to whom the whole command is addressed.

> "I the Lord do not change. So you, the descendants of Jacob, are not destroyed. Ever since the time of your ancestors you have turned away from my decrees and have not kept them. Return to me, and I will return to you," says the Lord Almighty. (Malachi 3:6-7)

The command to tithe is clearly to the descendants of Jacob only. This fact is also mentioned in the New Testament:

> Now the law requires the descendants of Levi who become priests to collect a tenth from the people — that is, their brothers — even though their brothers are descended from Abraham. (Hebrews 7:5, NIV)

Levites were commanded to receive tithes from their brethren, the other 11 tribes of Israel. They were also given the regulations of collecting the tithes and how to use these according to the law. Tithes were not to be collected from Gentiles (non-Jews).

Moreover, tithing is part of the Law of Moses and is among the numerous laws contained in the books of the law. We may therefore ask ourselves, which people were commanded to obey the law? When Moses went up the mountain to receive the tablets of stone, God's voice was clear about who He was sending him to for the purpose of delivering His covenant, with all the laws and regulations therein.

> Then Moses went up to God, and the Lord called to him from the mountain and said, "This is what you are to say to the house of Jacob and what you are to tell the people of Israel: 'You yourselves have seen what I did to Egypt, and how I carried you on eagles' wings and brought you to myself. Now if you obey me fully and keep my covenant, then out of all nations you will be my treasured possession. Although the whole earth is mine, you will be for me a kingdom of priests and a holy nation.' These are the words you are to speak to the Israelites." (Exodus 19:3-5)

It is beyond dispute, therefore, that the old covenant was never meant for all nations, but only for one very specific, chosen nation. We do not serve a God who is ambiguous, but one who is clear in His message and even whom every message applies to. Now contrast the instructions given to Moses, to speak to the children of Israel, with the message of Christ when He commissioned His disciples to preach the gospel:

> Therefore go and make disciples of all nations, baptizing them in the name of the Father and of the Son and of the Holy Spirit..." (Matthew 28:19)

Had God intended that the Law of Moses and its regulations and commandments should apply to people of all nations throughout the ages, surely He would have told Moses exactly that. He did not do so, leaving that sort of instruction only for the gospel of Jesus Christ. Unlike the law, the gospel is for both the Jew and the Gentile (Romans 1:16, Galatians 3:28).

The law cannot be obeyed piecemeal

As observed earlier, tithing is one out of numerous commandments and regulations contained in the Law of Moses. When God gave the law, He did not tell the Israelites to obey some of these commands and neglect others. Time and again He reminds them of their obligation to obey the whole Law:

> Keep all my decrees and all my laws and follow them. I am the Lord. (Leviticus 19:37)

> Moses and the elders of Israel commanded the people: "Keep all these commands that I give you today." (Deuteronomy 27:1)

In the New Testament, too, we are reminded that those who want to follow the law do not have the luxury they so often arrogate themselves to decide what regulations to obey and what to ignore:

> All who rely on observing the law are under a curse, for it is written: "Cursed is everyone who does not continue to do everything written in the Book of the Law." (Galatians 3:10)

Now, if anyone sincerely believes that God has commanded Christians to tithe, then that person is bound to obey all the regulations and commandments of the law. Selecting a few rules with a potential for financial gain and neglecting all the other decrees smacks of selfishness.

The tithe was all about food, not money

All the passages that address the command to tithe require the giving of food, not money. There was money at the time of Moses, Malachi and Jesus, yet only food is mentioned by all three.

> A tithe of everything from the land, whether grain from the soil or fruit from the trees, belongs to the Lord; it is holy to the Lord. (Leviticus 27:30)

> Bring the whole tithe into the storehouse, that there may be food in my house. Test me in this," says the Lord Almighty, "and see if I will not throw open the floodgates of heaven and pour out so much blessing that there will not be room enough to store it. (Malachi 3:10)

> "Woe to you, teachers of the law and Pharisees, you hypocrites! You give a tenth of your spices — mint, dill and cummin. But you have neglected the more important matters of the law — justice, mercy and faithfulness. You should have practiced the latter, without neglecting the former. (Matthew 23:23)

But how do we know that there was money as early as the time of Moses? The following passage is illustrative:

> Be sure to set aside a tenth of all that your fields produce each year. Eat the tithe of your grain, new wine and oil, and the firstborn of your herds and flocks in the presence of the Lord your God at the place he will choose as a dwelling for his Name, so that you may learn to

revere the Lord your God always. But if that place is too distant and you have been blessed by the Lord your God and cannot carry your tithe (because the place where the Lord will choose to put his Name is so far away), then exchange your tithe for silver, and take the silver with you and go to the place the Lord your God will choose. Use the silver to buy whatever you like: cattle, sheep, wine or other fermented drink, or anything you wish. Then you and your household shall eat there in the presence of the Lord your God and rejoice. (Deuteronomy 14:22-26)

Practices in the administration of tithing

There are numerous observances to do with tithing that modern preachers conveniently ignore. A few examples will do.

A penalty is levied if one is to tithe in cash. Anyone wishing to pay in cash ended up paying 12 per cent, not 10 per cent.

If a man redeems any of his tithe, he must add a fifth of the value to it. (Leviticus 27:31, NIV)

From this verse, one more issue comes out: Like in many societies around the world, men were accorded certain roles in the Israelite community that were not extended to women. Tithing and the priesthood were roles given to men. Advocates for tithing, if they had the least compassion for their flock, should then at the very minimum release women from this obligation. Due to their greed, however, they want to get a tithe of every household income, both from men and women.

The tithe was also to be given only from the tenth part, not the first. This is in contrast to what many advocates of the tithe teach, that one must give a tithe before doing anything else with their money. Any farmer with an increase of two or four or seven sheep, for instance, would not be expected to give any of them as a tithe.

> Every tithe of the herd and flock — every tenth animal that passes under the shepherd's rod — will be holy to the Lord. (Leviticus 27:32)

A tithe is not the same thing as 10 per cent. A tithe is the tenth part, not a percentage. An increase of 16 sheep, for instance, would necessitate a tithe of only one sheep (the tenth), not 1.6 sheep, which is the figure that counting as a percentage would lead to.

The third year of tithes was supposed to be given to the Levites, the alien, the fatherless and the widow. Naturally, pastors claim to be the New Testament Levites (with no scriptural sanction). Whatever the case, however, why do we not see them inviting, every three years, the other categories who together with them are supposed to partake of the tithe?

> When you have finished setting aside a tenth of all your produce in the third year, the year of the tithe, you shall give it to the Levite, the foreigner, the fatherless and the widow, so that they may eat in your towns and be satisfied. (Deuteronomy 26: 12)

The people themselves were to eat part of the tithe. Now, why don't our good sectarian leaders ever invite their congregants to share some of the tithe money they so aggressively ask for?

> Eat the tithe of your grain, new wine and olive oil, and the firstborn of your herds and flocks in the presence of the Lord your God at the place he will choose as a dwell-

ing for his Name, so that you may learn to revere the Lord your God always... Then you and your household shall eat there in the presence of the Lord your God and rejoice. (Deuteronomy 14:23-26)

The Levitical Priesthood only applied in the Old Testament

God appointed the Levites to take care of the worship at the tabernacle. They did not receive an inheritance, unlike the other 11 tribes of Israel, and were to be supported through receiving tithes from those other tribes. In turn, the Levites were to pay tithes to those among them who were priests (descendants of Aaron). The priests did not tithe.

The Lord said to Aaron, "You, your sons and your father's family are to bear the responsibility for offenses against the sanctuary, and you and your sons alone are to bear the responsibility for offenses against the priesthood. Bring your fellow Levites from your ancestral tribe to join you and assist you when you and your sons minister before the Tent of the Testimony.

The Lord said to Aaron, "You will have no inheritance in their land, nor will you have any share among them; I am your share and your inheritance among the Israelites.

"I give to the Levites all the tithes in Israel as their inheritance in return for the work they do while serving at the Tent of Meeting. From now on the Israelites must not go near the Tent of Meeting, or they will bear the consequences of their sin and will die. It is the Levites who are to do the work at the Tent of Meeting and bear the responsibility for offenses against it. This is a lasting ordinance for the generations to come. They will receive no inheritance among the Israelites. Instead, I give to the

Levites as their inheritance the tithes that the Israelites present as an offering to the Lord. That is why I said concerning them: 'They will have no inheritance among the Israelites.' "

The Lord said to Moses, "Speak to the Levites and say to them: 'When you receive from the Israelites the tithe I give you as your inheritance, you must present a tenth of that tithe as the Lord 's offering. Your offering will be reckoned to you as grain from the threshing floor or juice from the winepress. In this way you also will present an offering to the Lord from all the tithes you receive from the Israelites. From these tithes you must give the Lord's portion to Aaron the priest. You must present as the Lord's portion the best and holiest part of everything given to you.' (Numbers 18: 1-2, 20-29, NIV)

If we are to apply the Levitical model in today's church, then we ought to ask, Do we have New Testament Levites? Who are the New Testament priests? Who are the 11 tribes? To whom do those who claim to have taken up the Levitical position tithe? And do they, like the Levites, ensure they own no land – or, in our modern economy, no other source of income?

The New Testament says in no uncertain terms that the Levitical priesthood has changed, leading directly to the abolition of the written code of Moses (which includes the regulations on tithes).

If perfection could have been attained through the Levitical priesthood – and indeed the law given to the people established that priesthood - why was there still need for another priest to come, one in the order of Melchizedek, not in the order of Aaron? For when the priesthood is changed, the law must be changed also. He of whom these things are said belonged to a different tribe, and no one from that tribe has ever served at the altar. For it is clear that our Lord descended from Judah, and in regard to that tribe Moses said nothing about priests. And what we have said is even more clear if another priest like Melchizedek appears, one who has become a priest not on the basis of a regulation as to his ancestry but on the basis of the power of an indestructible life. For it is declared:

"You are a priest forever, in the order of Melchizedek."

The former regulation is set aside because it was weak and useless (for the law made nothing perfect), and a better hope is introduced, by which we draw near to God. (Hebrews 7:11-19)

Moreover, the New Testament states that all believers form "a royal priesthood" (1 Peter 2:9). We no longer need a human mediator between us and God, for the way to the Most Holy Place has now been opened.

Scripture does not create categories of priests in the New Testament. All those who have come to faith in Christ are now children of God with full benefits of sonship. Why would some priests, then, want to tithe to their fellow priests? Remember that even in the Old Testament, priests did not tithe.

Giving before the Law

(i) Abraham

It is often argued in favour of tithing that it existed even before the Law, the main example being Abraham's giving in Genesis 14. We need to first examine the relevant scriptures both in the Old and New Testaments carefully.

After Abram returned from defeating Kedorlaomer and
the kings allied with him, the king of Sodom came out
to meet him in the Valley of Shaveh (that is, the King's
Valley).

Then Melchizedek king of Salem brought out bread
and wine. He was priest of God Most High, and he
blessed Abram, saying,
"Blessed be Abram by God Most High,
Creator of heaven and earth.
And blessed be God Most High,
who delivered your enemies into your hand."

Then Abram gave him a tenth of everything. (Genesis 14:17-20)

This Melchizedek was king of Salem and priest of God
Most High. He met Abraham returning from the defeat
of the kings and blessed him, and Abraham gave him a
tenth of everything. First, the name Melchizedek means
"king of righteousness"; then also, "king of Salem"
means "king of peace." Without father or mother, without genealogy, without beginning of days or end of life,
resembling the Son of God, he remains a priest forever.
Just think how great he was: Even the patriarch Abraham
gave him a tenth of the plunder! (Hebrews 7:1-4)

It is important to note that Abraham gave from the spoils of
war, not his personal possessions. Again, we are not told that he
did so regularly.

Did Abraham give as a way of attracting blessings? From
the scriptures above, it is evident that Melchizedek first blessed
Abraham, after which he gave the king a tenth of the plunder.
He therefore did not give as a precondition for blessing. Neither
does God expect us to pay Him something or bribe Him before

He can bless us – even earthly fathers are more benevolent than that!

It is instructive that scripture says that Abraham gave – he did not pay. Abraham was not paying a debt but rather giving a freewill offering of his own volition. This means we cannot use Abraham's giving as a scriptural precedent for asking brethren to pay tithes.

Believers need also to get their principles of biblical interpretation right. The mere fact that someone did something in the Bible – however righteous that person is shown to be – does not constitute a command for Christians to do likewise. If we must give a tenth merely because Abraham did, then we may as well do the many other things that Abraham did, such as leaving our own countries to settle in distant lands, performing animal sacrifices and circumcising all male believers. And why not also put on sackcloth like David, walk barefoot and naked like Isaiah, let our hair grow like Samson's, and advise our young men to seek out adulterous women for marriage like Hosea did?

(ii) Moses

Apart from the giving of Abraham, we also have an example of the giving of Moses, who was actually commanded by God what proportion to give – also from the spoils of war:

> Divide the spoils equally between the soldiers who took part in the battle and the rest of the community. From the soldiers who fought in the battle, set apart as tribute for the Lord one out of every five hundred, whether women, cattle, donkeys or sheep. Take this tribute from their half share and give it to Eleazar the priest as the Lord's part. From the Israelites' half, select one out of every fifty, whether women, cattle, donkeys, sheep or other animals. Give them to the Levites, who are responsible for the

care of the Lord's tabernacle." So Moses and Eleazar the priest did as the Lord commanded Moses. (Numbers 31:27-30)

Although both Abraham and Moses gave from the spoils of war, it is clear that their giving was vastly different. If Christians are to follow Abraham's example, then they would give a tenth. If they are to follow the example of Moses, on the other hand, then people in the armed services would be expected to give 0.2 per cent, while ordinary citizens would give two per cent. Now, if we take it that the giving of a righteous man in the Bible constitutes a command for us to give in the same manner, why – apart from clear selfishness – would anyone insist that we must follow the example of Abraham and not that of Moses? This comparison between the giving of Abraham and that of Moses therefore buttresses the point that Christians are under no obligation to do something simply because someone in the Bible did it. We can only seek to replicate a Biblical precedent if it at the same time agrees with God's clear command to ourselves.

(iii) Jacob

The compulsion to pay tithes began with Jacob, the father of the twelve tribes of Israel. When he left Beersheba and headed for Haran, he made a stopover at Bethel where he spent the night and encountered God. He then made a vow:

Then Jacob made a vow, saying, "If God will be with me and will watch over me on this journey I am taking and will give me food to eat and clothes to wear so that I return safely to my father's house, then the Lord will be my God and this stone that I have set up as a pillar will be God's house, and of all that you give me I will give you a tenth." (Genesis 28:20-22)

From these verses, it is obvious why advocates of tithing prefer to concentrate on Abraham and in large measure ignore Jacob. What Jacob did was to give a conditional promise – he is to give a tenth only if God blesses him. This is unlike what is taught by many preachers that believers must give a tithe of every income they get, regardless of the measure of material provision they may have received or the challenges they may be going through in their lives at a particular time.

(iv) Joseph

After Joseph had interpreted his dreams, Pharaoh recognized that this was no ordinary man, but "one in whom is the spirit of God" (Genesis 41:38). When the famine foretold came to pass and the Egyptians had exhausted all their money and given their livestock, their land and even themselves in exchange for food from Joseph, he made a deal with them.

> Joseph said to the people, "Now that I have bought you and your land today for Pharaoh, here is seed for you so you can plant the ground. But when the crop comes in, give a fifth of it to Pharaoh. The other four-fifths you may keep as seed for the fields and as food for yourselves and your households and your children. (Genesis 47:23-24)

If tithing is such an important Biblical concept that many preachers are at pains to reassure believers that it existed even before the law, then why do we not see it anywhere else except as a one-time action by Abraham and no one else? Joseph would surely have demanded of the Egyptians to give a tenth in keeping with any such principle, yet we find him asking for twice as much!

The argument that tithing predates the law therefore falls flat on its face.

Jesus fulfilled the Law on behalf of those under the Law

It is often argued by advocates of tithing that Jesus said He did not come to abolish the Law. This is only partially true. The complete verse reads as below.

Do not think that I have come to abolish the Law or the Prophets; I have not come to abolish them but to fulfill them. (Matthew 5:17)

The key to understanding this verse, then, is to fathom what Jesus meant by the words "to fulfill them." Reading through the remainder of that chapter, we cannot fail to see that Jesus simply extricated the righteous requirements of God's law from the myriad regulations of the Mosaic Code. For certain laws (murder, adultery), His demands went even beyond the requirements of the Mosaic Law. He made adjustments to other regulations (divorce, for instance). He also completely abolishes others (oaths, revenge). Jesus is able to do what He wants with the law because He declares He is Lord of the Sabbath (and hence the Law).

Any Christian claiming that Jesus did not make any changes to the Law and that it is to be obeyed just as given by Moses will be bound to end up in a sea of confusion, for indeed One Greater than Moses did come and make a major clarification on the Law – by wrapping it all into the law of love.

Nobody could possibly fulfill the Law perfectly. Failing to satisfy the requirements of any of the many commandments attracted a curse. Jesus had to come, therefore, to fulfill the righteous requirements of the law on behalf of all those under the yoke of the law.

This explains why, throughout His life and ministry, we come across aspects of the Law of Moses that Jesus appears to consent to. After his birth, Mary the mother of Jesus went through "purification" according to the Law of Moses. On the eighth day, the baby Jesus was circumcised. Later, the parents took the young child to the temple to offer the sacrifices commanded in the Law (Luke 2:21-24). As a young boy, we see Jesus accompanying His parents on the annual pilgrimage to Jerusalem (Luke 2:41ff).

Later in His ministry, we find Jesus commending the Pharisees for their strict adherence to tithing, while castigating them for ignoring the weightier matters of the Law (Matthew 23:23). We also notice that Jesus told those whom He had healed of various illnesses to go to the priests and perform the sacrifices commanded by Moses for their cleansing (Mark 1:44). Our Master also observed the Passover (Luke 22:1-22).

We cannot pick out one of these incidents and use it to claim that Jesus approved of the practice; if we say He approved tithing, we must also accept that He approved animal sacrifices and pilgrimages to Jerusalem. The fact is that He was born under the Law and had to obey it – up to the time He died on the cross.

Having fulfilled the Law perfectly, Jesus does not require our help in further fulfilling it; on the contrary, the New Testament declares that even those who were under the law (the Israelites) are redeemed from it when they come to Christ.

> Christ redeemed us from the curse of the law by becoming a curse for us, for it is written: "Cursed is everyone who is hung on a tree." (Galatians 3:13, NIV)

The whole law was abolished at the cross

The defining moment of our salvation occurred at the cross when Christ died. Having fulfilled the Law, at the cross He abolished the written code.

When you were dead in your sins and in the uncircumcision of your sinful nature, God made you alive with Christ. He forgave us all our sins, having canceled the written code, with its regulations, that was against us and that stood opposed to us; he took it away, nailing it to the cross. (Colossians 2:13-14, NIV)

New Testament Giving

Tithing is not commanded anywhere in the Bible for New Testament believers. The early church and the apostles did not practise tithing. Christians are not called upon to tithe, but rather to give. Generosity is in fact encouraged.

Remember this: Whoever sows sparingly will also reap sparingly, and whoever sows generously will also reap generously. Each of you should give what you have decided in your heart to give, not reluctantly or under compulsion, for God loves a cheerful giver. (2 Corinthians 9:6-7)

Of course, stating a proportion that believers must give creates compulsion, which is expressly forbidden. Actually, in the New Testament we recognize that all that we have belongs to God; it is 100 per cent that is holy, not just 10 per cent. The example of the widow who gave all that she had (Luke 21:1-4) is pertinent.

We worship God all the days of the week, not merely on a Sabbath, or Sunday, or some other special days and seasons. We worship Him wherever we are and do not have to go to special man-made temples to do so. We are able to exceed the requirements of the Mosaic Code because the Spirit of God dwells within us. It is this Holy Spirit who tells us when, whom, where and how much to give. There is no formula or fixed proportion involved.

It should be noted also that in exhorting the Corinthians to give generously, Paul was not asking for funds to enable a personal luxurious lifestyle. The collections were meant to help the poor saints in Jerusalem (Romans 15:26). Paul worked to meet his own needs; indeed, even the exhortation that it is more blessed to give than to receive was addressed to elders (pastors) and not the ordinary flock (Acts 20:17ff). This shows that New Testament believers should all be prepared to bless one another: we do not have an exclusive category of givers and another of receivers.

Indeed, if ever there was an opportune moment for the early church to obligate believers to obey certain aspects of the Law of Moses, this was provided by the Council of Jerusalem (Acts 15). The Council was called to deliberate on whether the Gentiles should be made to obey aspects of the Law of Moses. After discussion, the Council was agreed that the Law of Moses was not to be applied on Gentile believers. Peter's words were particularly clear.

"Now then, why do you try to test God by putting on the necks of Gentiles a yoke that neither we nor our ancestors have been able to bear? No! We believe it is through the grace of our Lord Jesus that we are saved, just as they are." (Acts 15: 10-11)

Our faith is a response to God's grace. (Ephesians 2:8). We didn't try to impress God so as to save us. We were saved simply by God's grace. Anyone trying to be nice to God so as to be saved actually offends Him. Prayer and fasting, reading the Bible, going to Church, singing in the Choir, tithes and offerings, etc, do not buy us salvation. To the already saved, these practices don't make us more saved. Neither do we become less saved if we fail to do them. To fight guilt for our failings we normally resort to a list of things we must do to be "properly" saved or "restored" into salvation, tithing being one of them.

Believers spend much time and energy repenting even over things that God hasn't demanded, such as tithing. They cannot enjoy being in God's presence due to misplaced guilt.

God has given us eternal rest (Hebrews 4:9-11). We all do good works as we are enabled by God's grace already at work in us. We cannot buy favours from God. Rather, we use His grace to do good works as our worship and this enhances our fellowship with Him. If we did not pay anything for the great sacrifice of Jesus having to come and die for our sins, surely God will grant us the lesser things of this world without trying to obligate Him with tithes.

> He who did not spare his own Son, but gave him up for us all — how will he not also, along with him, graciously give us all things? (Romans 8:32)

Grace and greed do not go together. The gospel of giving according to the grace of God is virtually absent in many sects. Although Protestant Christians are taught that they are saved by grace, they are trained to give under the law: either the Law of Moses or that of their denominations.

Every Sunday, messages of condemnation are broadcast to millions of believers. The commonest of them is about tithing. That means a believer who has to fight tough spiritual wars on every front can no longer seek encouragement in the church gathering. These messages of condemnation lead to fear on the part of the believer that God no longer looks upon them favourably but sees them as robbers. Scripture shows us that such fear is unfounded and not from God.

The Spirit you received does not make you slaves, so that you live in fear again; rather, the Spirit you received brought about your adoption to sonship. And by him we cry, "*Abba,* Father." (Romans 8:15)

Harassed from all fronts - the family, workplace, neighbourhood, bills, name it – what today's believer badly needs is encouragement. Instead, he discovers that financial matters have a special place in the heart of the pastor.

In most denominations, the believer's commitment is gauged by tithing. Every member's tithing records are meticulously scrutinized. Normally, the faithful tithers end up in an informal club. Those outside this club are also informally discriminated against, a bad practice that destroys fellowship in the body of Christ.

God does not condemn and curse His children, He graciously rebukes them. God's aim is correction, not intimidation. Indeed, His Son did not come to condemn but to save (John 3:16-17). The era of the Law of Moses is over. Everything in the New Testament operates on grace and freedom in Christ as guided by His Spirit.

No one should be oppressed or discriminated against because of the amount they give. That is why all giving should be discreet, strictly between God and the believer.

Christians who are sensitive to the move of the Holy Spirit in their lives will give to bless others in the household of faith, to meet the needs of itinerary apostles, to help the poor and needy in society, to support evangelistic efforts and for any other purpose as the Lord directs. Any teaching that attempts to control and manipulate believers to give in a particular manner and to a specific person or institution, thus stifling the leading of the Holy Spirit, is to be rejected.

Chapter 12
False teachings: Abusing the blood of Jesus

It has become fashionable, in the prayers of many Christians, to invoke the blood of Jesus. The assumption is that special power or grace is obtained when the blood is called upon, regardless of the purpose for which this is done.

But the blood of Jesus is not like any other blood. Our very salvation was obtained at the cross. We should therefore be extremely careful to ensure that we do not deprecate or scandalize the cross through our words and actions. The cross and related imagery deserve our utmost attention in ensuring we have a proper understanding that leads to thankfulness to God and reverential worship to Him for the work accomplished at Calvary.

It cannot be in doubt that whenever the blood of Jesus is mentioned in the New Testament, the forgiveness of sins is in sight. Whether the immediate context is reconciliation with God, or purchasing the church of God, or redemption, or initiating a new covenant, the larger picture has to do with the forgiveness of sins. Below is a selection of some of these verses:

Then he took the cup, and when he had given thanks, he

gave it to them, saying, "Drink from it, all of you. This is my blood of the covenant, which is poured out for many for the forgiveness of sins." (Matthew 26:27-28)

God presented Christ as a sacrifice of atonement, through the shedding of his blood – to be received by faith. (Romans 3:25)

For he has rescued us from the dominion of darkness and brought us into the kingdom of the Son he loves, in whom we have redemption, the forgiveness of sins. (Colossians 1:13-14)

For this reason, Christ is the mediator of a new covenant, that those who are called may receive the promised eternal inheritance – now that he has died as a ransom to set them free from the sins committed under the first covenant. (Hebrews 9:15)

…To him who loves us and has freed us from our sins by his blood, and has made us to be a kingdom and priests to serve his God and Father – to him be glory and power for ever and ever! Amen. (Revelation 1:5-6)

Whenever anyone preaches, sings or writes of the blood of Jesus in the same vein as the New Testament writers, that person is moving in accord with scripture. Unfortunately, this is not always the case.

For selfish reasons, believers are asked to claim the blood of Jesus over things that are far removed from what the New Testament teaches. But the word of God only achieves the purpose for which the Lord has ordained, not what man thinks it ought to do:

"For my thoughts are not your thoughts,
neither are your ways my ways,"
declares the Lord.
"As the heavens are higher than the earth,
so are my ways higher than your ways
and my thoughts than your thoughts.
As the rain and the snow
come down from heaven,
and do not return to it
without watering the earth
and making it bud and flourish,
so that it yields seed for the sower
and bread for the eater,
so is my word that goes out from my mouth:
It will not return to me empty,
but will accomplish what I desire
and achieve the purpose for which I sent it. (Isaiah 55:
8-11)

Pleading the blood of Jesus over people, inanimate objects and animals

Many believers, as a matter of routine, claim the blood of Jesus over themselves, their homes, cars, roads in their area and even over their fields and animals. By such prayers, they seek protection against the schemes of the devil.

Christians have always rightly sought God's help from danger and persecution. It is also proper to seek Him for our material provision. In the New Testament, however, no Christian "covered" the road he was about to travel on with the blood of Jesus. They simply prayed for God's protection. Period.

Because we serve a merciful God who loves us despite our many weaknesses, He grants us the protection we crave for. It is not because of the blood of Jesus that He does this, but simply out of His grace.

Such misuse of the cross degrades its estimation among the community of believers and distracts from the work of the cross, since we come to treat the cross and the blood of Jesus as playthings to be tossed anywhere and anyhow we want.

Praying for the sick by means of the blood of Jesus

The phrase "By His wounds (or stripes in KJV) we are healed" is invariably used by many believers whenever the sick are prayed for. This phrase is employed by both Isaiah and Peter, the latter quoting the former. As with everything else in the study of scripture, we need to put it in the context in which it is used by these two writers:

> Surely he took up our pain
> and bore our suffering,
> yet we considered him punished by God,
> stricken by him, and afflicted.
> But he was pierced for our transgressions,
> he was crushed for our iniquities;
> the punishment that brought us peace was on him,
> and by his wounds we are healed.
> We all, like sheep, have gone astray,
> each of us has turned to our own way;
> and the Lord has laid on him
> the iniquity of us all. (Isaiah 53:4-6)

> "He himself bore our sins in his body on the cross, so that we might die to sins and live for righteousness; "by his wounds you have been healed." For "you were like sheep going astray," but now you have returned to the Shepherd and Overseer of your souls. (1 Peter 2:24-25)

From the context of the above passages, there can be little doubt that neither Isaiah nor Peter is referring to bodily healing. Preceding the phrase, "by his wounds we are healed," Isaiah writes about "our transgressions," "our iniquities" and "the punishment that brought us peace." Immediately after the famous phrase regarding healing, once again the prophet writes about "the iniquity of us all." How then can Isaiah be writing about physical healing, except by the most distorted logic?

The same goes for Peter. Before mentioning healing, Peter writes about Jesus having borne our sins on the cross. Immediately after writing about healing by his wounds, he again writes about straying sheep returning to their shepherd. That's all spiritual healing, with nothing remotely to do with physical wellbeing.

The New Testament shows us that Isaiah was also referring to physical pain in Isaiah 53:4, in addition to the spiritual angle implied by the context; this was however fulfilled during Jesus' ministry on earth alongside all other prophesies concerning the Messiah:

> When evening came, many who were demon-possessed were brought to him, and he drove out the spirits with a word and healed all the sick. This was to fulfill what was spoken through the prophet Isaiah:
>
> "He took up our infirmities
> and bore our diseases." (Matthew 8:16-17)

God was healing the sick long before the coming of Jesus on earth. By the hand of the prophets, he even raised the dead. He did not have to send His Son to the world in order to be able to do that. In our day, he continues to heal sickness in the same way that he did for millennia before the cross: By His grace and mercy. There is absolutely no need of bringing the cross and the blood of Jesus into the equation.

From the above discussion, one can see that whenever healing is mentioned in the bible, it does not necessarily refer to freedom from bodily illness. Quite often, the word of God is referring to spiritual healing. When we overturn the meaning intended by the word of God and supplant it with our own, we become no more than manipulators unworthy to be entrusted with the treasures of the kingdom.

Whenever the blood of Jesus is claimed for healing, it is certain that while healing will occur in some cases, in others this will not be the case. What happens in cases where the sick person still dies anyway? I would venture to suggest that the witness of the cross is much diminished to those around. If there are fifty-fifty chances of the blood of Jesus healing the sick, some may ask themselves, how sure can I be that it will wash away my many sins?

As mentioned earlier in this chapter, God cannot be coerced to perform according to our desires. When we use God's word to claim what His word does not promise, there is bound to be disappointment. He will still heal the sick according to His will, but will not do so just because we have prayed using the blood of Jesus. It is the witness of the blood of Jesus among humans that suffers in the process.

Praying for cleansing of the sins of believers with the blood of Jesus

This is perhaps the commonest error and is done almost universally, with few questioning the practice. Wherever Christians are gathered, it is almost guaranteed that one of the items for prayer will be a fervent cry for the Father to forgive the sins of those gathered, of course by the blood of Jesus.

Now, what could possibly be wrong about that? Well, everything, seeing that it is a totally unnecessary prayer. It is a prayer that betrays ignorance of one's position in Christ and the changes that take place at the moment of salvation. It shows a failure to understand the assurance of our salvation: that those who are truly born again are not subject to condemnation:

> Therefore, there is now no condemnation for those who are in Christ Jesus, because through Christ Jesus the law of the Spirit who gives life has set you free from the law of sin and death. For what the law was powerless to do because it was weakened by the sinful nature, God did by sending his own Son in the likeness of sinful humanity to be a sin offering. And so he condemned sin in human flesh, in order that the righteous requirement of the law might be fully met in us, who do not live according to the sinful nature but according to the Spirit. (Romans 8:1-4)

It is in the minds of many people that only past or confessed sins are forgiven. When the bible declares that our sins are forgiven, however, there is no indication that this refers to only a certain category of sins and that others have to be constantly repented on a daily or weekly basis. All sins are forgiven, not merely past sins or confessed sins. We do not serve a capricious God who gives eternal life and then takes the gift away every moment a Christian falls into some temptation.

> For he has rescued us from the dominion of darkness and brought us into the kingdom of the Son he loves, in whom we have redemption, the forgiveness of sins. (Colossians 1:13-14)

And if Christ has not been raised, your faith is futile; you are still in your sins. (Romans 15:17)

I am writing to you, dear children,
because your sins have been forgiven
on account of his name. (1 John 2:12)

This is why, even though Paul chastised the church of Corinth for its numerous shortcomings, he could still say that they were clean and did not require them to seek a second washing with the blood of Jesus:

Or do you not know that wrongdoers will not inherit the kingdom of God? Do not be deceived: Neither the sexually immoral nor idolaters nor adulterers nor male prostitutes nor practicing homosexuals nor thieves nor the greedy nor drunkards nor slanderers nor swindlers will inherit the kingdom of God. And that is what some of you were. But you were washed, you were sanctified, you were justified in the name of the Lord Jesus Christ and by the Spirit of God. (1 Corinthians 6:9-11)

Writing to the seven churches of Asia, the apostle John also implied that the cleansing by the blood of Jesus was a once-for-all affair rather than a continuous exercise:

To him who loves us and has freed us from our sins by his blood, and has made us to be a kingdom and priests to serve his God and Father – to him be glory and power for ever and ever! Amen. (Revelation 1:5b-6)

Repentance is for those outside the kingdom; once people come to Christ, they are declared free of the stranglehold of sin. That does not mean that believers will not err. It is simply an acknowledgment that God by His sovereign will has chosen not to take the sins of the righteous into account against them:

> Now to anyone who works, their wages are not credited to them as a gift, but as an obligation. However, to anyone who does not work but trusts God who justifies the ungodly, their faith is credited as righteousness. David says the same thing when he speaks of the blessedness of those to whom God credits righteousness apart from works:
> "Blessed are those
> whose transgressions are forgiven,
> whose sins are covered.
> Blessed are those
> whose sin the Lord will never count
> against them. (Romans 4:4-8)

> Who will bring any charge against those whom God has chosen? It is God who justifies. Who then can condemn? No one... (Romans 8:33ff)

If the Lord will never count the sins of a believer against them, it is not because of their many words of repentance every morning and evening. Simply, the Lord has determined NEVER to count the sins of the righteous against them. This should encourage the believer all the more to produce good fruit. The fact that our sins are not accounted against us is not an encouragement to go into sin. As Paul says, we ought to use our newfound freedom to do what is right. That freedom should never however be taken away, which is what daily repentance exercises do.

> You, my brothers and sisters, were called to be free. But do not use your freedom to indulge the sinful nature; rath-

er, serve one another humbly in love. (Galatians 5:13)

The bible teaches that all the sins of the believer have been washed away, once for all. They are not washed little by little as they are confessed upon being committed. If that were so, then it elevates our own works; it would be a way of declaring that grace alone is insufficient. Depending on one's level of spiritual maturity, believers may not even realize that certain things are sinful, say for instance the unscriptural division of the body of Christ by following spiritual leaders of our choice (see Paul's rebuke in 1 Corinthians 1:10-13). Since such a sinful disposition would have remained unrepented throughout the believer's lifetime, does it preclude such a person from going to heaven? Of course not: Even the person who accepts Christ on their deathbed and has no time to read any verse in the bible to know what is acceptable or unacceptable to God will still enter paradise.

Behind the logic of frequent repentance is fear of displeasing God. But the word of God exhorts us not to fall into this snare:

The Spirit you received does not make you slaves, so that you live in fear again; rather, the Spirit you received brought about your adoption to sonship. And by him we cry, *Abba,* Father." (Romans 8:14-15)

The writer to the Hebrews makes a fitting analogy between the ministry of Christ and that of the earthly priests before him. In chapter 7, he shows us that unlike earthly priests, Jesus is able to save completely:

Now there have been many of those priests, since death prevented them from continuing in office; but because Jesus lives forever, he has a permanent priesthood. Therefore he is able to save completely those who come to God through him, because he always lives to intercede for them. (Hebrews 7: 23-25)

That's an astonishing claim: Jesus is able to save completely. That means those who come to him are saved once and for all time. They cannot be saved today but in need of some prayers to make them purer tomorrow.

In chapter 9, the writer to the Hebrews says that while the earthly priests entered the temple regularly to perform their ministry, Christ only suffered once for all:

For Christ did not enter a sanctuary made with human hands that was only a copy of the true one; he entered heaven itself, now to appear for us in God's presence. Nor did he enter heaven to offer himself again and again, the way the high priest enters the Most Holy Place every year with blood that is not his own. Otherwise Christ would have had to suffer many times since the creation of the world. But he has appeared once for all at the culmination of the ages to do away with sin by the sacrifice of himself. (Hebrews 9:24-26).

In the next chapter, this writer then points out that the sacrifices offered according to the law were imperfect since they could not cleanse once for all in the manner that the sacrifice of Christ had done:

The law is only a shadow of the good things that are coming – not the realities themselves. For this reason it can never, by the same sacrifices repeated endlessly year after year, make perfect those who draw near to worship. Otherwise, would they not have stopped being offered? For the worshippers would have been cleansed once for

all, and would no longer have felt guilty for their sins.
(Hebrews 10:1-4)

The question then arises: If sacrifices that must be repeated endlessly are so worthless as this passage implies, and the
perfect sacrifice (of Jesus) cleanses once for all and makes the
worshippers no longer feel guilty, why would any Christian feel
the obligation to undertake the worthless sacrifice of continuous
repentance that does not remove guilt permanently? Where guilt
has been taken away once for all by the blood of Jesus, why
would anyone need to continuously go on their knees begging
for mercy? There would be no difference between such a person
and the Old Testament worshippers described by the writer of
the letter to the Hebrews. If anything, Hebrews is categorical
that such sacrifices are no longer necessary:

Day after day every priest stands and performs his religious duties; again and again he offers the same sacrifices, which can never take away sins. But when this
priest had offered for all time one sacrifice for sins, he
sat down at the right hand of God, and since that time
he waits for his enemies to be made his footstool. For by
one sacrifice he has made perfect forever those who are
being made holy.
    The Holy Spirit also testifies to this. First he says:

"This is the covenant I will make with them
after that time, says the Lord.
I will put my laws in their hearts,
and I will write them on their minds.

Then he adds:

"Their sins and lawless acts
I will remember no more."

And where these have been forgiven, sacrifice for sin is
no longer necessary. (Hebrews 10:11-18)

Although the writer to the Hebrews was referring to the
temple animal sacrifices conducted by the Aaronic priesthood as
compared with the blood of Jesus, his argument would apply to
any man-made effort or regulation regarding the forgiveness of
sins. In that case, since the blood of Jesus makes the worshipper
perfect once for all and forever, it is actually a sign of unbelief
and offensive to God to keep seeking what He has already so
graciously given.

And because our own petitions for cleansing can never take
away sins, our witness of the power of the blood of Jesus is destroyed by such prayers. The blood cannot be that powerful, it
may be argued, if it has to be used to cleanse us again and again.
What of the danger that one may forget or not have the opportunity to cleanse themselves just before death?

What then becomes of our guilt when we know that we have
done something displeasing to God? You should thank God pro-
fusely that by His grace even that sin has been forgiven, reject the
enemy's attempts to bog you down with accusations, determine
to have a better walk in the Spirit by hiding yourself in Christ
more than ever before, wipe off the dust and move on with the
battle. If other brethren are to help out, they should do so by
sharing your burden through counseling, material assistance and
prayer for your strengthening. There should be no condemnation
and no prayers for cleansing by the blood of Jesus.

Because we have not attained perfection, we are to help in
restoring one another and in mutual strengthening to overcome
our faults. Once restoration is accomplished for a brother or sis-

ter who was going astray, we rejoice that the child of God has realized their mistake and we continue marching on together against the enemy. God's love, however, is never diminished upon any of His children for any reason, nor does the brethren being restored need any sinner's or repentance prayers. No more misuse of the blood of Jesus.

It is only when we accept the biblical position that we have been cleansed once for all that all worries are put to rest. We can then experience the full joy of our salvation without constant worries about what sin we may have forgotten to repent, or if we overlooked repenting last night, or any other such anxieties born out of a misunderstanding of the scriptures. We can only enter God's rest and thus experience true peace if we have rested from our many works:

> There remains, then, a Sabbath-rest for the people of God; for those who enter God's rest also rest from their own work, just as God did from his. Let us, therefore, make every effort to enter that rest, so that no one will perish by following their example of disobedience. (Hebrews 4:9-11)

We know that the Old Testament was "only a shadow of the good things" (Hebrews 10:1). The rest spoken of in the New Testament is not rest from physical work, although this is often desirable as well. God is always at work and never rests, or else the devil would finish us all. The true rest accorded by the gospel is cessation from our own works in pursuit of perfection and righteousness. When we refuse to enter that rest by preferring our own efforts at purification, the passage above indicates that we are then following in the Israelites' example of disobedience. The writer to the Hebrews warns his readers of the dire consequences of failing to enter God's rest: They will perish, just as the Israelites did. If we must day after day say prayers of repentance, we can hardly be said to have entered that rest.

Christ knows our weaknesses. He has saved us despite those imperfections, of which as the Creator He is fully aware:

> But we have this treasure in jars of clay to show that this all-surpassing power is from God and not from us. (2 Corinthians 4:7)

> For we do not have a high priest who is unable to empathize with our weaknesses, but we have one who has been tempted in every way, just as we are – yet he did not sin. (Hebrews 4:15)

If Christ knows our weaknesses so intimately and is ready by His grace and mercy to forgive sins, then there must be another reason for having destroyed the Israelites who were in the wilderness with Moses, not just their actions arising out of mere human weakness:

> See to it, brothers and sisters, that none of you has a sinful, unbelieving heart that turns away from the living God. Who were they who heard and rebelled? Were they not all those Moses led out of Egypt? So we see that they were not able to enter, because of their unbelief. (Hebrews 3:12, 16, 19)

Those who have believed the message of Christ are able to go before God despite their weaknesses, knowing that our loving Father has accepted them in that imperfect condition:

> Let us then approach God's throne of grace with confi-

dence, so that we may receive mercy and find grace to help us in our time of need. (Hebrews 4:16)

It is impossible to approach the throne of grace with confidence if Christians are preoccupied with thoughts about whether they are really worthy to go before the Father. That is an indication of unbelief – they do not believe that God has accepted them despite their many weaknesses. In sectarian thinking – where some people imagine that God's presence is more pronounced at the front – they will want to hide at the back of the congregation.

It is good to remember that, "Jesus Christ is the same yesterday, today and forever." (Hebrews 13:8) Unbelief is detestable before God. It essentially denotes a lack of faith, without which "it is impossible to please God." (Hebrews 11:6) When scripture affirms in no uncertain terms that all our sins are forgiven once and for all, yet believers find that they must seek cleansing by the blood of Jesus every now and then, the sin of unbelief is as much in our midst as it was among the followers of Moses who were destroyed.

The forsaking of useless rituals, including repentance prayers that serve no purpose, is an elementary matter that believers ought to have learnt and embraced long ago. However, because of focusing on physical rather than spiritual phenomena, and because their priesthood has been so severely assaulted by false apostles, they still need to be reminded of the basics of their faith:

Therefore, leaving the elementary message about the Messiah, let us go on to maturity, not laying again the foundation of repentance from dead works, faith in God, teaching about ritual washings, laying on of hands, the resurrection of the dead, and eternal judgment. (Hebrews 6:1-2, CSB)

There is much in the world waiting to be changed by our prayers. Satan is extremely pleased when, instead of going on an all-out attack against him, we instead engage our energies on examining ourselves and doubting whether we are truly pleasing to God, hence the need for constant repentance prayers. When we truly believe that our salvation has not come about by our own efforts but is the result of the grace of God, then we can get rid of all such distractions and follow the Lord's leading into the battlefield. When Christians do this, Satan's days would have been numbered.

Chapter 13
False teachings: Assorted practices

W e will now examine, briefly, a few more false doctrines and practices. The aim, as stated earlier, is not to go through all false teachings, but merely to look at some of the serious false teachings of our day. In the process, the pattern will be clear that false doctrines merge the spiritual with the physical, a logical development that would have started right from water baptism.

Anointing oil

In the Old Testament, anointing oil was mainly used to consecrate priests and kings. It was also used to consecrate sacred grounds and articles used by the priesthood (see, for example, Exodus 29-30).

Like the rest of the regulations contained in the Law of Moses, the use of anointing oil should be taken to have been abolished in the New Testament. Its continued use, say in James 5:14, can only be understood as a hangover from Judaism and not as Christian practice. Note also that the letter by James was addressed, "To the twelve tribes scattered among the nations," which means that this apostle was writing to the Jewish Diaspora, who would have had vestiges of Jewish practice in their Christian lives.

The use of anointing oil in the 21st century, and particularly olive oil, can best be understood as a sinister business orchestrated by ruthless false apostles to fleece unsuspecting and ignorant brethren. Some of these messengers of Satan masquerading as apostles of Christ also use elements such as water and soil. Of course, many well-meaning Christian leaders and their followers sometimes use these elements due to ignorance.

The New Testament anointing has nothing to do with human activity. It is God who anoints His people:

Now it is God who makes both us and you stand firm in Christ. He anointed us, set his seal of ownership on us, and put his Spirit in our hearts as a deposit, guaranteeing what is to come. (2 Corinthians 1:21)

As for you, the anointing you received from him remains in you, and you do not need anyone to teach you. But as his anointing teaches you about all things and as that anointing is real, not counterfeit – just as it has taught you, remain in him. (1 John 2:27)

As usual, it is the human weakness to believe what is seen with the physical eye that makes people seek to anoint and be anointed with physical oil. That points to serious spiritual malady.

Sectarianism

Sectarianism, or the unscriptural division of the church, is perhaps the biggest cancer afflicting the body of Christ today. A large section of Christians have become so spiritually numb that they see nothing wrong with their modern church practices as far as the gathering of believers is concerned. Although the bible is unambiguous in its message, it is a testimony of man's inability to accept God's ways that people will seek to change what it says to suit themselves, or to conveniently ignore it altogether.

The first four chapters of 1 Corinthians are dedicated to rebuking the Corinthians over their carnality in following apostles of their liking rather than focusing on Christ. The New Testament does not sanction the division of believers not only with regard to spiritual leaders, but also on the basis of nationality, economic status, spiritual maturity, gifting, teaching or any other ground save locality.

Unscriptural division of the body of Christ occurs because of man's desire for control based on an inability to trust the Holy Spirit's leading. But there is a warning about the price to pay:

If anyone destroys God's temple, God will destroy that person; for God's temple is sacred, and you together are that temple. (1 Corinthians 3:17)

This verse makes it as clear as it can ever get that the church is not an institution of men to be run according to our ways. We must find out how God wants His temple to run and fit in with that plan. The alternative is destruction, because we will be working against God's purposes while pretending to do His work.

The church is God's family of saints; it has nothing to do with buildings and organizations. While many Christians may agree with this statement, in actual practice they insist on structures and hierarchical organizations.

With this in mind, it should be obvious that denominationalism has no place in Christianity. Neither Jesus nor the apostles ever set up any denomination or system of religion, the fraudulent claims by the Roman Catholic Church to have been established by the apostles notwithstanding.

Within the assembled gathering, the bible assigns to every believer an equal role and does not create an upper caste of Christians to micro-manage the church:

> What then shall we say, brothers? When you come together, everyone has a hymn, or a word of instruction, a revelation, a tongue or an interpretation. All of these must be done for the strengthening of the church. (1 Corinthians 14:26)

There is no central command in the true church. No church is under the direction of any other church, nor is there any such thing as a national or international church. Individuals with an apostolic anointing may, however, have a ministry that involves travelling to many nations for the purpose of planting and strengthening churches. The New Testament church is not an organization but a living organism, with Christ as the sole, invisible head.

In the true church, there is no such thing as offices – what many believers often call "the five-fold ministry offices of apostle, prophet, evangelist, pastor and teacher." These are only gifts. There is absolutely no use of titles.

Oratorical ability is not a sign of spirituality. Gathering large crowds may show organizational prowess, but this was quite unnecessary in the early church as the believers met in homes. Paul wrote firmly against the "super-apostles" of his day who were expert orators and sought to gather huge crowds to themselves for purposes of self-enrichment. On the contrary, he spoke the word of God free of charge:

FALSE TEACHINGS: ASSORTED PRACTICES

Was it a sin for me to lower myself in order to elevate you by preaching the gospel of God free of charge? I robbed other churches by receiving support from them so as to serve you. (1 Corinthians 11:7-8)

It was not out of poverty, persecution or small numbers that the apostles failed to build magnificent temples for Jesus. None of these factors has ever stood in the way of those who have erected such structures in later generations. It was because the priesthood of the believer is diluted in large gatherings, since such congregations cannot enable individual participation. Those who are weak in the faith, in particular, will simply melt into the crowd, never to mature spiritually.

Moreover, when the mentality of bigger is better kicks in, funds tend to be allocated for grandiose purposes that do not agree with God's will. When believers in Jerusalem sold their goods and brought the money to the feet of the apostles, the funds were used to meet the needs of believers, not construction projects. And when the Grecian widows complained about being neglected in the distribution of food, the apostles went to the extent of appointing seven men "full of the Holy Spirit" to ensure they were well catered for.

When the focus is to enlarge attendance, to have more money coming in and to constantly plan for projects, the biblical focus of helping the poor among us is completely lost.

There are many other important characteristics of the New Testament church that a careful study of the scriptures reveals. These suffice, however, to illustrate the general nature of the New Testament church and the far the denominational system has deviated from this model. The net effect of sectarianism and a wrong conception of church is sad indeed. We have ended up with large crowds in huge cathedrals, but the spiritual state of these multitudes is one of deep slumber.

Spiritual Covering

This false doctrine is designed to completely control and manipulate the believer. The teaching has absolutely no scriptural warrant. Basically, this teaching holds that every believer must have the spiritual covering of another believer, say the pastor, who then has a covering of their superior, and so on going upwards.

The doctrine of spiritual covering fails to take account of New Testament teaching that hierarchical relationships are now anathema to the people of God.

When the mother of the sons of Zebedee made a request for her children to take the places of honour in Jesus' kingdom, the Lord used the occasion to make his teaching known regarding top-down relationships:

> Jesus called them together and said, "You know that the rulers of the Gentiles lord it over them, and their high officials exercise authority over them. Not so with you. Instead, whoever wants to become great among you must be your servant, and whoever wants to be first must be your slave – just as the Son of Man did not come to be served, but to serve, and to give his life as a ransom for many." (Matthew 20:25-28)

Three chapters later, Jesus on yet another occasion taught his disciples regarding this matter as he warned them not to become like the teachers of the law:

> "But you are not to be called 'Rabbi,' for you have only one Master and you are all brothers. And do not call anyone on earth 'father,' for you have one Father, and he is in heaven. Nor are you to be called 'teacher,' for you have one Teacher, the Messiah. The greatest among you

will be your servant. For those who exalt themselves will be humbled, and those who humble themselves will be exalted. (Matthew 23:8-12)

There is no precedent in the New Testament for believers to look up to anyone on earth for spiritual covering. This doctrine seeks to destroy direct communion between the believer and God by planting a human mediator in between. But the priesthood of every believer and God's desire to speak directly to each of His children cannot be denied:

Let us then approach God's throne of grace with confidence, so that we may receive mercy and find grace to help us in our time of need. (Hebrews 4:16)

Spiritual covering, then, is an affront to the priesthood of every believer. And once the believer's priesthood has been so thoroughly assaulted, he cannot but become a limp Christian who merely follows the denominational instructions given. That cannot be the plan of God.

Chapter 14
True baptism without legalisms

T he counterfeit will always seek to displace the genuine. The secret to staying on the right course is not to expend time and energy in discovering the details of each and every falsehood that rears its ugly head, for these will keep coming up all the time. We ought, instead, to immerse ourselves in the truth so much that we get to know the genuine intimately. Then, whatever the devil tries to bring up – it doesn't matter how the lie manifests itself – we will instantly recognize and expose his counterfeit handiwork.

True baptism is the work of God in uniting Himself to those He freely calls. That way, we become one body with His Son, Jesus Christ, and are joined together in this body with all others whom He has chosen to share in this life. No man can purport to create this unity for himself or others – the power of God alone creates and sustains this unity.

This becomes clear if we pursue the whole witness of scripture rather than isolated verses picked out of context. When we isolate verses from their context and from the overall message of scripture running right through the bible, we end up distorting spiritual realities and justifying our own denominational biases and traditions. This is as true of water baptism as it is of any other church traditions.

A believer who has been baptized into Christ and nurtured in good soil will easily understand that spiritual realities belong to a totally different realm from the physical world and elements; that he is called to walk not by what he can see, but by his new belief in Christ Jesus; and that only the spiritual reality is of eternal value.

The believer who is made to understand from the beginning the spiritual nature of his union and relationship with God would have started on an excellent footing. Other believers can only praise God and thank Him for the salvation of the new believer without purporting to add any other essentials, for none are possible. No sinner's prayer is necessary. No water baptism is called for. Membership cards have no place in this union with God. Neither are denominational ties necessary or even desirable. Communion with God and fellowship with other Christians does not require any such preconditions.

The tree of such spirituality will produce obvious fruit. Such fruit is bitter to those who are steeped in human tradition but sweet to any who want to enjoy their freedom in Christ. If a believer is truly united with Christ, and this spiritual union is maintained by the power of God, who is Almighty, then the believer will not have the mentality that he has "fallen" if he does not do what others prescribe with their traditions, because Christ says of those He saves that, "No one can snatch them out of my Father's hand." (John 10:29) He will do good as God enables and directs, but such a believer will also recognize that finally it is not our acts of righteousness that matter, however good these may be, but only the grace of God.

Because direct union and communion with God is a reality, the believer will assert his priesthood. He will not travel across hills and mountains to seek the power of God from some televangelist, because he knows that this power is available to him also wherever he is. He will recognize that his own prayers are as powerful as any other believer's. Hence, he will not fall prey to the circuses of "deliverance," "miracle healing," "seed planting" and other misadventures that modern-day false teachers have invented to mint money from ignorant faithful.

A believer grounded in true spirituality understands that because He is one with the Lord wherever he may be, he does not need to visit some physical "house of God" out there in order to be in the presence of God. He understands that the temple built by Solomon was a mere shadow of the things to come; he himself is not similarly required to put up a physical building, for Christ dwells in Him and believers are the true temple of the Holy Spirit. He knows that it is believers who are holy, not inanimate objects such as buildings, water and oil. Practices bordering on the superstitious, often using physical elements, will not attract him.

This sort of Christian will go to the gatherings of believers wherever they are held with the attitude of seeking fellowship, not to passively hear from a certain "man of God," as if he himself were incapable of hearing from the Lord. He will constantly want to humble himself and not seek his own glory but Christ's. At gatherings, this means he will not seek to dominate but rather to allow Christ to minister freely to all present through whomever He wishes. Anyone who tries to sneak in suspicious teachings at such gatherings will be rebuked by believers eager to maintain their freedom in Christ, because they will be well grounded in the truth.

Since he has humbled himself, the believer planted in good spiritual soil will take the attitude of John the Baptist: "He must become greater; I must become less." He will not seek titles, honour and praise from men. On the contrary, he will want to identify with the meek and lowly, that they too may feel at home with other believers and not be intimidated in any way, such that they would fear to express what Christ wants to say or do through them. Such a Christian therefore realizes that spiritual gifts of whatever nature do not confer hierarchical authority, but are merely meant for service to one another. Neither do spiritual gifts confer any right to burden others with demands for financial or other support; on the contrary, greater gifting calls for an even higher level of humility in ensuring that one becomes an example to others of the importance of hard work, generosity, perseverance in adversity and all other virtues.

Because he recognizes that his union with Christ is sustained by the power of God Himself, this radically different Christian cannot be confused into believing that physical rituals or substances can have any eternal value. He knows that when Jesus commanded his disciples to wash one another's feet, He was not initiating a ritual but asking them to take care of one another's needs in love. Similarly, he also understands that when Jesus asked the disciples to take bread and wine in memory of him, he was not instituting a ritual, as though food has any eternal value in the kingdom; rather, He was asking them to share their lives with one another. It is in the memory of Jesus and to His glory when believers share their joys and sorrows, physical needs and provision. It is not the physical washing of feet and sharing of unleavened bread and wine that is pleasing to God, but actual communion and fellowship in every form. To reduce the essence of Christ's message to rituals and legalisms is offensive to the very message of the gospel that is being preached.

Baptism in Christ is only the beginning of the believer's walk. From start to finish, the discerning believer must be careful not to be deceived by the almost identical but counterfeit paths that the enemy lays in an attempt to make him deviate from the one that leads to the city that God has prepared for His people (Hebrews 11:16). Following in the example of his master, he must be prepared for ridicule and persecution. That means he must not be keen on the approval of men or seek strength in numbers; on the contrary, whenever he sees a well-trodden path, he will need to remember the caution Jesus gave:

> Enter through the narrow gate. For wide is the gate and broad is the road that leads to destruction, and many enter through it. But small is the gate and narrow the road that leads to life, and only a few find it. (Matthew 7:13-14).

In this spiritual journey, he must never forget that the letter kills, but the Spirit gives life (2 Corinthians 3:6).

Bibliography

Alexander, T.D. and Rosner, Brian S., *New Dictionary of Biblical Theology*, InterVarsity Press, UK, 2000.

Atkerson, Steve (Editor), *House Church, New Testament Reformation Fellowship*, US, 2008.

Berkhof, Louis, *Systematic Theology*, The Banner of Truth Trust, US, 1958,, 2005.

Brauch, Manfred T., *Abusing Scripture: The Consequences of Misreading the Bible*, InterVarsity Press, US, 2009.

Brown, Michael L., *Revolution in the Church: Challenging the Religious System with a Call for Radical Change*, Chosen Books, US, 2002.

Bubeck, Mark I., *The Adversary: The Christian Versus Demon Activity*, The Moody Bible Institute, Chicago, US, 1975.

Bubeck, Mark I., *Overcoming the Adversary: Warfare Praying Against Demon Activity*, The Moody Bible Institute, Chicago, US, 1984.

Carrier, Marc, *The Gospel According to Jesus: Unwrapping Centuries of Confusion*, Kingdom Expansion Series, Values-Driven, 2010.

Cole, Neil, *Organic Leadership: Leading Naturally Right Where You Are*, Baker Books, US, 2009.

Culver, Robert Duncan, *Systematic Theology: Biblical and Historical*, Christian Focus Publications Ltd, UK, 2005.

Davidson, Ivor J., *The Birth of the Church: From Jesus to Constantine, AD 30- 312*, Volume 1 of The Monarch History of the Church, Monarch Books, Oxford, UK, 2005.

Elwell, Walter A., *Evangelical Dictionary of Theology*, Baker Academic and Paternoster Press, UK, 1984, 2001.

Erickson, Milard J., *Christian Theology*, 2nd Edition, Baker Academic, US, 1998.

Fee, Gordon D. and Stuart, Douglas, *How to Read the Bible for All Its Worth*, Zondervan, Michigan, US, 2003.

Fortenberry, Jack, *Corinthian Elders*, Bridgepointe Publishing Company, Brandon, 2008.

Green, Michael, *Evangelism in the Early Church*, Hodder and Stoughton, London, UK, 1978.

Grudem, Wayne, *Systematic Theology: An Introduction to Biblical Doctrine*, InterVarsity Press, UK, 1994, 2005.

Hendriksen, William, *The Gospel of Matthew, New Testament Commentary*, The Banner of Truth Trust, UK, 1973, 1989.

Hill, Jonathan, *The History of Christian Thought: The Fascinating Story of the Great Christian Thinkers and How They Helped Shape the World as we Know it Today*, InterVarsity Press, US, 2003.

Ing, Richard, *Spiritual Warfare*, Whitaker House, US, 1996.

Kraft, Charles H., *Confronting Powerless Christianity: Evangelicals and the Missing Dimension*, Chosen Books, 2002.

Lloyd-Jones, D. Martyn, *Authority*, InterVarsity Press, London, UK, 1958, 1976.

Marshall, I. Howard (Editor), *New Testament Interpretation*, The Paternoster Press, US, 1992.

Nee, Watchman, *The Normal Christian Church Life: The New Testament Pattern of the Churches, the Ministry, and the Work*, Living Stream Ministry, Anaheim, US, 1980, 1994.

Patzia, Arthur G., *The Emergence of the Church: Context, Growth, Leadership and Worship*, InterVarsity Press, 2001.

Pierce, Ronald W. and Groothuis, Rebecca Merrill, *Discovering Biblical Equality: Complementarity without Hierarchy*, InterVarsity Press, US, 2005.

Prior, David, *The Church in the Home*, Marshall Morgan and Scott, UK, 1986.

Ramm, Bernard, *Protestant Biblical Interpretation* (Third Revised Edition), Baker Books, US, 1970.

Reid, Daniel G. (Editor), *The IVP Dictionary of the New Testament: A One-Volume Compendium of Contemporary Biblical Scholarship*, InterVarsity Press, Illinois, US, 2004.

Renwick, A.M. and Harman, A.M., *The Story of the Church* (Third Edition), InterVarsity Press, Leicester, UK, 1958, 1999.

Snyder, Howard A., *New Wineskins: Changing the Man-made Structures of the Church*, Marshall, Morgan and Scott, London, UK, 1975.

Thoman, Roger, *Simple/House Church Revolution*, Appleseed Publications, US, 2008.

Turner, Max, *The Holy Spirit and Spiritual Gifts Then and Now*, Paternoster Press, Cumbria, UK, 1996.

Viola, Frank, *From Eternity to Here: Rediscovering the Ageless Purpose of God*, David Cook, US, 2009.

Viola, Frank, *Pagan Christianity: The Origins of Our Modern Church Practices*, Present Testimony Ministry, 2002.

Viola, Frank, *Reimagining Church: Pursuing the Dream of Organic Christianity*, David C. Cook, Colorado, US, 2008.

Viola, Frank, *Rethinking the Wineskin: The Practice of the New Testament Church*, Present Testimony Ministry, 2001.

Virgo, Terry, *Restoration in the Church*, Kingsway Publications Ltd, Sussex, UK, 1985.

Walker, Andrew, *Restoring the Kingdom: The Radical Christianity of the House Church Movement*, Hodder and Stoughton, London, UK, 1985.

Willmington, H.L., *Willmington's Guide to the Bible*, Tyndale House Publishers, Illinois, US, 1981, 1984.

www.ingramcontent.com/pod-product-compliance
Lightning Source LLC
Chambersburg PA
CBHW060759050426
42449CB00008B/1458